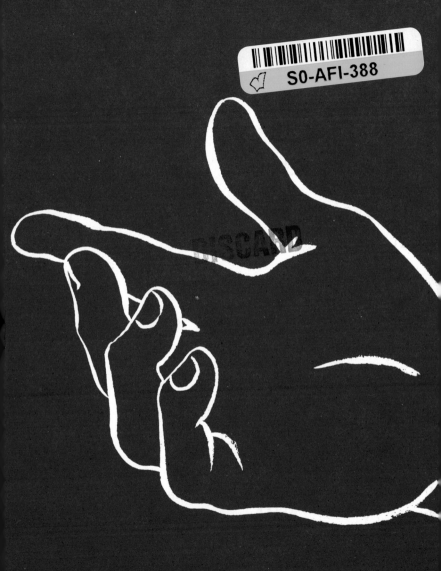

UNHELPFUL
BEHAVIOR

SIX HOURS LATER

NOTICE

UNHELPFUL
BEHAVIOR

THIRTY MINUTES LATER

NOTICE

UNHELPFUL
BEHAVIOR

THE NEXT DAY

NOTICE

UNHE-
BEHA-

NOTICE

-LPFUL
-VIOR

TRIGGER ⇨

NOTICE

UNHELPFUL BEHAVIOR

HELPFUL BEHAVIOR

IF YOU'RE FREAKING OUT, READ THIS

A coping workbook for building good habits, behaviors, and hope for the future

SIMONE DeANGELIS

Foreword by FAITH G. HARPER
PHD, LPC-S, ACS, ACN

Microcosm publishing
Portland, OR

IF YOU'RE FREAKING OUT, READ THIS

A Coping Workbook for Building Good Habits, Behaviors, and Hope for the Future
© Simone DeAngelis, 2020
Introduction by Dr. Faith G. Harper
First edition © Microcosm Publishing, 2020
ISBN 978-1-62106-901-0
This is Microcosm #199
Edited by Cynthia Marts
Cover and Design by Joe Biel
Illustrations by Simone DeAngelis

For a catalog, write or visit:
Microcosm Publishing
2752 N Williams Ave.
Portland, OR 97227
www.Microcosm.Pub

To join the ranks of high-class stores that feature Microcosm titles, talk to your rep: In the U.S. Como (Atlantic), Fujii (Midwest), Book Travelers West (Pacific), Turnaround in Europe, Manda/UTP in Canada, New South in Australia, and GPS in Asia, India, Africa, and South America.

If you bought this on Amazon, we're so sorry because you could have gotten it cheaper and supported a small, independent publisher at Microcosm.Pub

Global labor conditions are bad, and our roots in industrial Cleveland in the 70s and 80s made us appreciate the need to treat workers right. Therefore, our books are MADE IN THE USA.

Library of Congress Cataloging-in-Publication Data

Names: DeAngelis, Simone, author.
Title: If you're freaking out, read this : a coping workbook for building good habits, behaviors, and hope for the future / Simone DeAngelis.
Description: First edition. | Portland, Ore : Microcosm Publishing, [2020]
Identifiers: LCCN 2019021972 (print) | LCCN 2019981508 (ebook) | ISBN 9781621069010 (paperback) | ISBN 9781621060697 (ebook)
Subjects: LCSH: Adjustment (Psychology) | Mental health. | Self-help techniques.
Classification: LCC BF335 .D434 2020 (print) | LCC BF335 (ebook) | DDC 158.1--dc23
LC record available at https://lccn.loc.gov/2019021972
LC ebook record available at https://lccn.loc.gov/2019981508

MICROCOSM·PUBLISHING

Microcosm Publishing is Portland's most diversified publishing house and distributor with a focus on the colorful, authentic, and empowering. Our books and zines have put your power in your hands since 1996, equipping readers to make positive changes in their lives and in the world around them. Microcosm emphasizes skill-building, showing hidden histories, and fostering creativity through challenging conventional publishing wisdom with books and bookettes about DIY skills, food, bicycling, gender, self-care, and social justice. What was once a distro and record label was started by Joe Biel in his bedroom and has become among the oldest independent publishing houses in Portland, OR. We are a politically moderate, centrist publisher in a world that has inched to the right for the past 80 years.

OPENING LETTER

Dear Reader,

I f you are freaking out right now, the most important thing to know is that you are not alone in your suffering. If you think you are, you have more to learn. You are connected in this moment to all of those who have suffered in the same way. Your suffering is not unique, and that can be healing if you allow it to be. Breathe.

There are moments where you are just freaking the fuck out. Freak outs look different for everyone. For some it's self-harm, for others it's throwing plates, uncontrollable tears, and impulsive text messages. Sometimes it's suffering quietly. It is alright to have these moments. Everyone does. No one is one-hundred percent chill all the time. Not even you.

The ten coping skills that open this book are the tools that have worked very well for me in dealing with freak-outs, and they might work for you, too. The purpose of these coping skills is to get you to a place where you are able to feel and express your emotions in a productive way.

This book compiles the many great coping skills I have learned from my teachers, therapists, mentors, and peers, so that you can have them to refer to when you need it. I also try to bring hope and illustrate concepts by sharing how I handle pieces of my life.

Each chapter includes space to keep track of the skills that work best for you. Take these skills and explore ways in which you can apply them to your own life, so when you're freaking out, you can read this.

—*Simone*

THIS BOOK IS DEDICATED TO

Mi Tia,
Te amo. Kind, strong, resilient, patient, true.

TREVS FOREVS

BECAUSE OF YOU,

Mary,
   You helped future Sim
choose life. This all
started with you.

AVANI,
   You showed me what
kindness looks like. It
was years of darkness. And
then I saw kindness.
Thank you

TEN COPING SKILLS

1. BREATHE: Inhale. Exhale. This is what surviving looks like. Breathe.

2. MOVE: Your body is amazing. It does cool stuff. Move it.

3. REACH OUT: Humans are for each other.

4. SAY, "THANK YOU": Invite gratitude to the chaos party.

5. SHOWER: Thoughtful & mindful self-care.

6. SAY, "I LOVE YOU": Give yourself the approval you seek.

7. WRITE: Observe, get curious, learn, grow.

8. THINK ABOUT HOW COOL YOU ARE: pretty fuckin' cool.

9. RELAX: Create focused peace & intentional rest.

10. CONNECT WITH YOUR WORLD: Sometimes scary. Always nice.

you're doing a great job.

SAY ANY WEIRD STUFF YOU WANT: 1800 273 8255 ♥

Contents

FOREWORD: DR. FAITH G HARPER PhD, LPC-S, ACS, ACN

There is a story I first heard on *The West Wing* that I share with my clients regularly. My version is as follows:

A person falls into a deep black hole. It's dark. And damp and creepy and smelly and scary AF. They scratch at the dank, muddy sides of the walls for awhile but make no progress. They start screaming "Help me, please help me!" from the depths of the hole.

A doctor walks by, hears the screaming, and peers down. The doctor is worried about their stuckness and wants to help. They write out a prescription and toss it down into the hole. This doesn't get the stuck person too far in getting out of the hole. So they yell some more. "Help me, please help me!"

A minister, walking by, hears them and peers in. The person is excited and relieved that someone new has arrived and the minister is obviously very worried about their stuckness. The minister writes out a prayer for the stuck person and throws it into the hole. The prayer is comforting. And even appreciated. But it doesn't change their stuckness. They start yelling again. "Please! Stop throwing things down to help! I need *out*!"

Then a friend walks by and hears the screaming. They bend down and see the stuck person's tear-stained face peering back up at them. "Holy shit! You fell in the hole! Hold up a second." And then *they jump down into the hole*. The stuck person starts to freak out. "Why did you do that? Why?? You jumped down in here with me? Now we're *both* stuck!"

"Nah," the friend replies. "Because I've been down here before. And I know the way out."

There is a phrase we use in academia to describe this: lived experience. It's a shorthand way of talking about individuals who have been through some fucked up shit, therefore have a unique and empathic connection to whatever fucked up shit you are going through. They are often able to communicate their own experiences of both falling in and of getting out. Their map may not be exactly the same as yours, but chances are it's going to be pretty damn useful in charting your own course. They know the territory pretty damn well, so they point out the rough terrain. And the lurking monsters.

That is what Simone has created here. She shares the stories we don't hear in "polite" conversation. The stories to which we attach shame and stigma. As if there is shame to be associated with the struggles of being a human being in pain. But lived experience is not interested in the shame and stigma game.

There are lots of great tools out there, but none of them, unfortunately, are the One True Path™ to healing for everyone (and, holy shit, run like hell if anyone tries to convince you otherwise). Limiting ourselves to one specific type of tool is just dumb, but most self-help books unfortunately do just that. And having eleventy hammers is all well and good, unless you are in dire need of a socket wrench. Sim has been through a lot of treatment, and is here to share the tools she found most efficacious from various methods. So you get to try out some cool tips and tricks from Dialectical Behavior Therapy (DBT), Acceptance and Commitment Therapy (ACT), Mindfulness Based Stress Reduction (MSBR) and the like. (And yes, I'm totally blowing the dog whistle for my fellow clinicians wondering if this is a good book to recommend to clients.)

The point is, lived experience says "Fuck hiding our pain. There are holes all over the damn place. And if no one else is going to acknowledge all these holes, then I will. Here's my map. Maybe it will be helpful in developing yours. Let's stop ignoring all these damn holes, what do you say?"

If you are reading this, it's because you are in a hole. Or someone you care about is. And when you're freaking out, you don't need worthless pieces of paper flung down at you. You need help actually getting out. Let Simone climb down in with you, share her story about her own fall, and help you out.

—*Faith*

INTRODUCTION

When I wrote this book for the first time, it was ten pages long. I did not think anyone would ever see it. On each page, I wrote a note to myself explaining a coping skill that I knew I liked. On the cover I wrote, "if you're freaking out, read this."

That book was for future me, to give her something from someone who knows her really well—past me. Rational Simone knows what to do when shit hits the fan. So she wrote this book for the Simone who sometimes needs a reminder of how to feel without *becoming* her feelings.

Ultimately, I wrote this book for you.

This is not one of those books where I am promising that your life will change if you take these simple steps. I have no idea what will happen in your life and you do not need to try anything that does not sound cool. I do not and cannot know what is best for you or what will work for you.

Here are the things that inform what is in this book: over ten years of therapy, including six months of some intense therapy and life skills, continued psych care, and a deep love of authors whose books have changed the way my brain works.

The ideas in this book are my interpretation of the way I have synthesized and soaked up information over the years. I am deeply appreciative to all of the people who have been a part of that journey, whether they know it or not.

I am not an expert. My story is not particularly special, and I am not above-average anything. I am a person who struggled a lot. I got help, tried a bunch of new skills, and I changed my behaviors and my relationships, and the way I see the world. I wrote this book because I could not find anything out there that felt like it was written directly to me, by someone who also struggles with the hurricane of life.

I can't remember when I started thinking about the value of my life. It was early. I was traumatized and doing terribly in school. I attempted suicide for the first time when I was ten years old. I'd realized that life is nothing: in the scheme of the universe, in the scheme of the world, my problems didn't matter. My life didn't matter. These days, the idea that life is nothing opens up a lot of free space in which to build my very own life's meaning and purpose. At the time, the concept of nothingness completely fucked me up.

And who could I go to that would take me seriously? I didn't even have the vocabulary to identify what I was feeling or thinking. The following years of depression and some serious self-harm were fueled by the idea that I was too privileged to be sad and too insignificant to stay alive. There was trauma and tragedy, love and friendship.

The first time I went to a psychiatric hospital, I was fourteen. I was sent there because I told my therapist about my suicide plan for that night. It was an intensely heavy and dark atmosphere. No one was helpful, in fact the staff was rude. The truth is, some psych hospitals are scary and uncaring. I stayed for three nights and then convinced my mom to bail me out. After those three days, I decided to never go back to a place like that, and I decided to never tell anyone about my suicidal plans again.

I graduated high school and went to college with every intention to party the entire time. I stopped taking my meds, I didn't have a therapist, and my family was states away. I was free.

Two months into it, I was loving self-harm. A year into it, I started planning my suicide.

Eight months later, I was back in Austin for a summer visit and helped myself to a shit ton of wine and narcotics at my parents' house. I thought they were not home. They were definitely home.

At some point in the madness, I told my dad I wanted to die. The next day, we were in my childhood therapist's office. He was so sad and emotional. My parents were all on edge. They insisted I attend a psychiatric hospital. I agreed to go. They said it would be four weeks, everyone was really sad, it sounded like it would be nice to have all my problems solved for me (turns out, solving problems involves my own hard work). I figured that at the end of it, I would kill myself, and my family would feel like they had done everything they could.

During my last week before entering psychiatric care, I enjoyed my last days of freedom by partying *hard*. My friends surrounded me almost the entire time. They were worried. One night, I had hours of alone time and I harmed myself, badly. Two days later, May 31st, 2012, I entered psychiatric care. I was twenty.

I stayed in an inpatient hospital for nine weeks, then in the outpatient program for four-ish months. This place was not at all like the first one. The campus was beautiful, welcoming, calm. The staff was compassionate, understanding, and patient. I felt safe for the first time in my life. It was the most free I had ever felt. I got to find out what living a "meaningful life" really means to me.

Until I started really working through trauma and mental illness, every memory was tinted a bit darker. When I saw the past I only saw resentment and shame. I couldn't see through the trauma. I still have days when I feel sad about the way I spent the first twenty years of my life. And because of this work, I most frequently have days when I am full of gratitude and sunshiney love. Well, not always with the sunshiney love. Most of the time I'm just grateful that I am content. These are the days that make the hard work worth it.

In the years since leaving the psychiatric hospital, I have used wonderful tools I picked up from all the generous people who have shared with me. Many of these tools helped me make my own decisions about my life and whether or not to experience it.

Everything you will read comes from years of processing and navigating the existential crisis that has been my entire life. This is not a memoir. However, the only thing I can do is speak from my experience. This is what worked for me. Old behaviors and habits that directed my life were changed when I tried something new. I am going to talk about those behaviors and the things I did to make them more productive.

Every chapter comes back to **coping** with difficulty regulating emotions, starting with one of the most reliable skills and exploring others from there. Each section looks at different coping options, with space for you to work out your own version of each. Give yourself permission to imagine new skills, or old ideas, in a new way.

These coping skills, accompanied by stories and advice, are bits and pieces of my journey. The core principles behind all of these primarily revolve around gratitude, mindfulness, self-compassion, and authentic connections with others. I am not saying that the skills I present are the *best* coping skills ever for every single person; We are all different, and we handle the bullshit life throws at us differently. These are things I have learned that have made me joyful to the very core, even on the darkest of days.

I hope you try the coping skills nestled in the pages of this book that resonate with you, and I hope among them you find a few that work for you.

SHOW YOUR SELF

WHAT WILL YOU DO INSTEAD?

What would **I** do?

I = My most authentic, value-driven, compassionate self.

I = The person I am when I realize I am responsible for healing the hurt that was never my fault.

I = The person I am when I let fear connect me to others instead of push them away.

I = The person I am when I wholeheartedly love myself.

I = The person I am when I do not feel the need to control how I am perceived.

I = The person I am.

ONE : BREATHE

You might feel like this moment is unbearable. Maybe your thoughts feel suffocating and inescapable. You can begin to reach a level of calm by breathing.

Oxygen is good for your brain and it can help you feel peaceful. So, try giving your brain some oxygen now.

Start by simply noticing your breath.

Say,

"NOW I **INHALE,** NOW I **EXHALE.**"

You don't need to do anything else. You don't even need to be done freaking out.

Next, you can try a few things to bring more attention to your breath:

KEEP BREATHING

TRY THESE EXERCISES FOR MINDFUL BREATHING

Inhale through your nose for three seconds
exhale through your mouth for four seconds
inhale through your nose for five seconds
exhale through your mouth for six seconds

REPEAT THREE TIMES

---

inhale through your nose for as long as you can
fill your lungs completely
exhale all at once, like a big sigh

Lie down, put your hand on your stomach
expand your stomach as you inhale through your nose
Let your stomach fall as you exhale slowly

SQUARE BREATHING

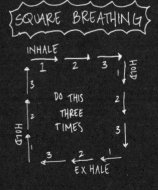

INHALE
1 2 3
HOLD
1
DO THIS THREE TIMES
2
3
HOLD
3 2 1
EXHALE

ACCEPT PEACE

Please accept any peace you begin to feel. With every breath, release the tension in your body as you notice it. You're doing great.

Take A Moment to Breathe

You are a functioning member of this world.

By being here you are participating. And that's enough. There isn't a way to live life exactly right. There just isn't. That is not a thing that exists. So, breathe yourself into the moment.

When you breathe, pay close attention to the oxygen flowing through your body. Imagine it going through your brain, giving you peace. You can breathe normally and simply pay attention to your breath. Or you can take big, deep breaths in through your nose and out through your mouth.

THERE IS SOMETHING YOU NEED TO KNOW, WHILE YOU ARE BEING.

YOU DO NOT HAVE TO BE GRAND TO BE WORTHY.

breathe.

IT'S LIKE BEING STUCK IN A FINGER-TRAP.

YOU CAN'T GET OUT BY FORCING ANYTHING.

breathe

I hope you try the coping skills nestled in this book, and I hope among them you find a few that work for you.

Remember Your Oneness

Breathing presents a special opportunity to hold a space for whatever peace you might need in each moment. The moment you realize you are not present is the purest moment of awareness. From there, breathe.

If you begin by noticing your breathing for five minutes each day, you will see the ripple effect of calm presented in your life. A daily meditation practice can make it easier to remember your breathing in moments of calamity.

Take a second right now. Hold this book, read this sentence as you inhale: *I am inhaling self-compassion.* Now exhale: *I am exhaling compassion.* Open your chest and relax your shoulders. Give your Self breath. Give your Self love. Give others breath. Give others love.

In this moment, when you hold in your heart deep compassion for every person, you are connecting your Self to the greater breath of the strange existence we are all a part of.

YOU DON'T HAVE TO BELIEVE IN ANYTHING TO CONNECT TO THIS. LET IT BRING YOU COMFORT.

LIFE IS
WEIRD SOMETIMES
(ALL THE TIME),

WHEN IT FEELS
LIKE TOO MUCH,

HERE'S WHAT I DO:

I TRY WITH CARE
& ATTENTION to
BREATHE MY WAY
TOWARD ACCEPTANCE.
"LIFE IS WEIRD," I SAY,
LIKE AN OBSERVATION
INSTEAD OF LIKE
A FRUSTRATION.

Draw your personal or emotional demons drinking tea with you.

Consider this a moment of truce. The darkness has no agenda.

Remember to drink your tea one sip at a time.

Sit With Depression

Depression is scary, and I don't hate it anymore. On days that I wake up and I don't feel its tight, suffocating grip on my mind, I sit with peace. I get grateful for the ease of getting out of bed. And I also try to celebrate *without* saying "that motherfucker is gone!" Because I am tired of talking shit to myself about my depression. It isn't bad. It isn't good. It just, very simply, is. And when I allow it to be, I can better hear what it wants to tell me.

"Sit with me, have tea" is a wonderful buddhist concept that encourages you to invite all of your fears and demons to sit with you and enjoy a peaceful cup of tea. By doing this, you are separating yourself from your negativity and treating it with compassion. I know that's hard, and you can also just imagine doing it, even if you can't quite get there yet.

You can practice this concept by visualizing your depression as a form. Usually I imagine it as basically a shadowy bigfoot. A giant beast, moping around like a raincloud. Not scary or mean, just there. You can picture your depression as separate from yourself. Picture sitting with it at a little table, quietly drinking tea. You are sharing a peaceful moment. I frequently do this visualization while drinking a cup of tea. I invite my anxiety, PTSD, self-centeredness. We sit together and we have tea. Nothing needs to be said, nothing needs to be resolved. You are just here, having tea. (side note: Do not imagine anyone or anything that might trigger you; invite what you are *ready* to sit with for tea.)

When I listen, I am grateful for my depression. It forces me to be authentic. To be honest. Because I know that over time, if I hide it, it grows. So I have to let it be seen. To let it be heard. And I try so hard not to hate it. "Sit with me," I say, "have tea."

It's okay to struggle and rumble and figure shit out. It's also okay to not be *able* to figure shit out.

I have come to understand that my depression was built into my brain a long time ago and it was triggered in order to protect me the very best way it knew how—to shut me off. To turn on my auto-pilot. To keep me from the moment, because there were moments that were too scary to be present for. So, my depression kept me away from what was going on. And now, it comes and it goes and it comes and I let it be. I try so hard to let it breathe.

Depression also helps me connect. Because when it comes, I know it's time to hold on tight to the people who love me and see me and who have my back. Depression is a survival mechanism that no longer serves me. I can hold it, or let it go to hold on to what is sturdy and true—community, truth.

When you're freaking out, it's like getting caught in an undertow. You're swimming and diving into the waves on a beautiful day, and then the wave takes you. And you didn't know that was coming, so you didn't quite have time to take a breath. In those situations, you need to relax. Don't exert energy by fighting it. You're in it, here it is. If you have the opportunity to breathe, take slow, deep breaths. Take the lifeguard's hand when they reach for you. Breathe.

Like driving through heavy fog, you can only see the ground three feet in front of you. Nothing to the side, nothing straight ahead. Try to find the line on the road and driveslowly, like a Texan in the rain. Breathe.

When I realized that my pain is bearable, I felt both free and terrified.

What are some truths that you can simply acknowledge as reality?

1.

2.

3.

4.

Examples:
- My friend is gone
- I failed that exam
- I am not in control of their life

Radical Acceptance

Radical acceptance is a tool to help you be *in* the moment and accept reality, in order to begin to overcome negative feelings about it. This is a Dialectical Behavior Therapy (DBT) concept that entails acknowledging that a situation did indeed happen. That's all. And it's harder than it might sound, depending on the intensity of the situation.

DBT is an excellent therapeutic practice for anyone who struggles with regulating emotions (i.e, all of us, at one point or another). This model of healing was developed by Dr. Marsha Linehan and it has worked wonders for those who practice it consistently. It helped me take a step back to observe my behavior, and accept the things I cannot control.

Radical acceptance means that you say, "Yes, this thing happened. It did indeed happen." You never have to be okay with it. You do not have to forgive. You are stating a fact, with no judgment attached to it.

This can bring up a lot of feelings that are great to talk to a qualified professional about. If you can't do that, reading some books you might relate to, practicing coping skills, and writing about it (if that sounds cool to you) can help you in a big way. There are also a bunch of free support groups that can help guide you in the right direction and give you a space to really *be*.

It's amazing how much simply acknowledging that your past did indeed happen can help you move forward. The facts of the situation are true. Yes. That does not mean you are happy about it. That does not mean you have forgiven all the way. It does not even mean that you think it was "for the better." I learned a ton about how to do this from Tara Brach, a brilliant woman who wrote a book called *Radical Acceptance*. That book is a game-changer.

Practicing radical acceptance does not at all mean that you are cool with what happened or is happening right now. It means you acknowledge that what is happening is actually happening, and what has happened did happen. That's all. By consistently practicing this concept, you can learn to look at your past objectively, in a way that does not trigger you the way it once did.

I promise there is joy to be found in the darkness. You do not have to wait for the pain to end to find it.

"THIS IS OXYGEN"

Set reminders on your phone, write yourself a note, think of it randomly throughout your day.

PRACTING THESE SKILLS WHILE YOU ARE NOT FREAKING OUT WILL HELP YOU COME TO AWARENES WHEN YOU are FREAKING OUT.

CONVERSATIONS WITH FEELINGS

BY ASKING QUESTIONS, YOU MIGHT LEARN MORE ABOUT WHAT YOUR FEELINGS ARE SHOWING YOU.

WHAT QUESTIONS DO YOU HAVE FOR YOUR FEELINGS?

QUESTIONS FOR MY _____
PLEASANT FEELINGS

QUESTIONS FOR MY _____
UNPLEASANT FEELINGS

TWO: MOVE

WHEN YOU FEEL LOST IN YOUR MIND, FIND YOUR BODY

No matter your current state of movement motivation, awareness of your body can help you come to a present moment that isn't horrible.

(AS)

So, try taking ten (or eleven, if you like odd numbers) steps. Slowly bend your knee, touch your heel to the ground, then your toe. Move your arms along slowly, or keep them still by your side.

* INSTEAD OF WALKING, YOU CAN CHOOSE ANOTHER SIMPLE MOTION TO REPEAT MINDFULLY. WHATEVER IS RIGHT FOR YOU.

MINDFULLY MOVING

As you take each step, breathe.

One step at a time, bring your
focus to each movement in each
s l o w step.

OR:
SLOWLY MOVE YOUR ARMS UP & DOWN
CLENCH & RELEASE FISTS
LIFT & RELAX YOUR EYE BROWS
ROTATE YOUR ANKLES IN CIRCLES

Feel Your Body

Grounding yourself is really difficult to do in times of weirdness or confusion. Take a moment to sit up and open your chest. Do a quick body-scan. Check your toes, feel your knees, relax your hips, drop your shoulders. Come into yourself. Check in with your Self.

Try doing a physical activity that you enjoy which boosts your mood. Take a five minute dance break. Masturbate and give yourself a great orgasm. Join a local recreational sports team. Engaging in physical activities that you enjoy will inevitably boost mood and provide a safe bubble to go to as needed.

Take Ten Steps

Some people are super into walking right now. I am all about reaching my step goals. What if it's not about the quantity of the steps, but about the quality of them? Out of your ten-thousand steps, how many were you acutely aware of?

How many times did you truly notice the way your foot feels when it hits the ground? How many times did you align your breathing with your walking?

Sometimes when I focus on my walking too much, I get very self-conscious. Am I walking correctly? Are people noticing my scoliosis?

Are my knees weird? So, I like to do mindful walking around my apartment or at the dog park when no one is there.

Focus on eleven steps, five steps, whatever.

Go Outside

On a walk through the city, spend three minutes with your head up, your headphones off, and slow everything down. Notice your breath, notice (one at a time) the colors you see. Relax your face into a small, peaceful smile.

While you hike in the mountains, stop to study the plants. Look up popular birds before you go, and try to identify them on your walk. Bring binoculars.

If you're walking down the beach, take your shoes off and focus on making those footprints in the sand. Push your heel in, roll your foot forward, bend your toes a bit longer than usual, take your next step.

Wherever you are, if you can, find a patch of grass or stones or water, and take your shoes off. Spend ten minutes with your feet on the ground, come back into your body. Bring your Self into your breath. Do this everyday.

Cross a Room

Set a timer for one hour. No matter how large or how small your room is, walk from one wall to another. Walk in one direction, one time. Take the entire hour.

Become aware of your body and your surroundings. Listen to any noises. Start a timer and start with standing. Do a body scan, relax and notice each part of your body, from your toes to your scalp. Take one, slow step. Notice your heel on the ground, your knees bending, your posture.

Just as in meditation, your mind will wander, you may get impatient. Simply observe yourself and non-judgmentally come back to the exact moment where you are. See what comes up for you.

Write or talk about it afterward. It can be an interesting experience

Working Out Feels Better

The first time I got a gym membership, I sat in the parking lot for thirty minutes and then drove home.

Finally, I told myself, "Sim, you only have to walk on the treadmill for ten minutes, that's all." That seemed manageable, so I did. And it worked. You don't need to do more than that. You don't need to go do all the weights if you don't know how to do them. You don't need to work out for an hour and get really sweaty.

If you go to a new yoga class and are nervous, remind yourself to get there early so you can get situated. Tell yourself, "Hey, you can lay down the entire time or you can skip a pose when you feel too fatigued. Do your best to remain present." Taking that pressure off is a nice relief.

Some days, maybe you'll walk on the treadmill for ten minutes and then go home. If on those days you leave the gym a little bit disappointed, give yourself the win because you actually walked into the gym and did something. It really does feel good, and it makes it that much easier to go back.

One thing that really helps me get motivated to go to the gym is remembering the feeling I get after I have given my body movement. Deeply visualize the feelings after a great time of physical engagement. Just thinking about that can begin to outweigh your desire to stay in bed or to organize your bookshelves again.

ENJOY MOVEMENT

WHAT ARE THREE SONGS THAT REALLY GET YOUR BONES GROOVIN' AND GET YOU MOVIN'?

1.

2.

3.

WHAT PHYSICAL ACTIVITIES DO YOU ACTUALLY ENJOY?

(CIRCLE SOME!
ADD YOUR OWN!)

surfing

yoga

sex

DANCE BREAK!

skiing

martial arts

walking dogs

jumping on the trampoline

1.

2.

3.

THREE: REACH OUT

call/text/message/whatever a person you
like and ask them to talk on the phone or
in person or through text(text is okay,
especially if they're reading as you're
sending).

Speaking with someone outside of this
situation can help with anxiety and
aloneness.

The way you feel is the way you
feel. You do not have to be alone
while you experience your feelings.

"THIS IS WHERE I AM"

IF YOU'RE NOT SURE WHAT TO SAY, HERE'S A
SCRIPT TO GIVE YOU SOME IDEAS...

"Hey/Howdy/Sup, _____ Can we talk about
(THEIR NAME)

a freak out I'm experiencing?"

THEM: "YES."

"Cool. What I need from you is _____
(WHAT YOU NEED -- JUST LISTEN,

_____. I am currently having
VALIDATE, ENCOURAGE, NOT ADVICE, ETC.

the feeling(s) _____. Something
(EMOTIONS/"I DON'T KNOW")

really pushed my freak out button. Here
is my situation... _____"
(EXPERIENCE TO THIS POINT)

Practice saying yes

T hink of every new social interaction as practice. Try to see what it feels like to get comfortable, to remain present and open.

Saying "yes" to new social opportunities can be difficult. Over time, it gets more comfortable. When you say yes, you meet new people.

Once there was a very cool woman I wanted to be friends with. She invited me to an event, and I said yes, knowing that she would be the only person there that I knew.

I got there thirty minutes before she did. First, I went to the bathroom and sat in the stall for a second to gather a game plan, tell myself I'm awesome, and do some power poses. After a few minutes (I don't care if everyone thought I was pooping), I went into the party and started approaching groups of people and just randomly joining their conversations. That's how you make friends, right?

The first two groups I approached were pretty awkward about it. That didn't stop me. In every situation, I learned. I didn't need to walk up to a group of laughing people and fake laugh at a joke they knew I didn't hear.

That night, I met another woman who I totally connected with, and we became friends. She introduced me to another cool woman, and we also became friends! So, I went to this event with one friend, and left with three. Not bad, if I do say so myself.

Every situation is recon. You go in, you do your best, you observe, and you have fun. After the interaction, think about what went well and what felt good and authentic for you. Imagine how you could do more of that and less people-pleasing in the future.

Making new connections and going places where you don't know anyone can feel really weird a lot of the time. Sometimes you have off nights. Whatever. Sometimes it goes really well and you have a lot of fun.

Talking (or Not) About Trauma

S ometimes the word "trauma" makes me feel uneasy, and words dealing specifically with traumatic experiences often make me feel even more uneasy. In this section, I did my best to avoid directly triggering words, and use the term trauma as a catch-all for the things that have hurt us in our lives.

When I addressed my trauma out loud with another person for the first time, I began feeling a little bit freer. So when I began talking about my trauma, I started talking about it a lot. I thought that in order to be authentic I needed to be 100% open to 100% everyone. As a result, I learned when it is and is not appropriate to talk about trauma.

As I have talked about my trauma over the years, I find myself talking about it less and less. That isn't because I want to hide it,

I think it's because I have come to identify with it less. When I think about those memories, I most often don't feel an immediate emotional response anymore. That's not to say that there haven't been days where I can't leave my house because going outside scares me. However, I can go a year or more without having one of those days (it really depends on the year).

I always thought that if I felt better, my life wouldn't have any more problems. And that just isn't the case. Talking about it helps.

Because despite the darkness, despite the shame, despite the nightmares—there is beauty, there is light, there is strength.

There are a couple of things you can do to help you embrace all of the light in your life. Connecting with others is the biggest one.

You never need to defend or explain your experience. And almost everyone I have ever said anything about trauma to has been nothing but supportive and loving, even if they were uncomfortable. It all depends on the feeling of safety for everyone in the conversation. It's totally up to you. It's your story, you do not have to share it when you do not feel safe. Being authentic does not require sharing anything that you do not feel comfortable sharing. When I talk about and process my trauma with professionals or close friends, I feel a sense of relief; another level of acceptance. I found key people who I can turn to when I have had a PTSD episode, or just a really bummer day when I can't get it out of my mind.

When you want to connect with someone and you end up talking about rough life experiences, don't directly tell the story or any details about specific events. Whew, I learned that lesson the hard

I have found that what frees me the most from the burden of my shame is saying things aloud to another person. Put the truth on the table, and see what happens.

way. Sometimes, even just talking about your own trauma can trigger another person's trauma, so make sure you're in the right environment and that everyone is cool with it.

It can be easier to talk about your trauma in a predictable situation, where it is understood that the topic is about to change and it's going to be okay. It is most comfortable when everyone involved in the conversation is ready to hold a space for trauma. Most of the time, this happens in therapy. However, you might also grow comfortable having these conversations with your close support people.

Bonus tip: When you talk about your trauma, make sure that you'll have time to finish the conversation with closure and positivity. If you're in the last 15 minutes of a coffee date, you might ask to not go there quite yet and save it for a day when you can give yourself all the time you need.

Keep an updated list
of people you can call
or text!

TIP: Sending a group text to a few people
can be easier. Say, "can any of you talk
right now?"

Mind Reading Only Seems Easier than Communication

My depression came to the forefront when I was ten, and it took until I was twenty to finally learn to admit I was struggling *before* I was in a crisis. I used to just wait until an especially bad suicide attempt or a major emotional breakdown. The habit was to smile and wave my way through my depression. I wanted other people to rescue me by reading my mind.

Maybe the biggest disappointment I ever realized was that people *can't* read minds. It was also the most uninformed assumption I have ever made. When I dated boys, I would think, "If he doesn't get me flowers today, it means he doesn't love me," and I never actually said anything about flowers out loud, ever. And then I would be pissed at the end of the day when I didn't get flowers. I used it as evidence of that fact that I was totally unloveable.

This desire for others to read my mind was true on a much bigger scale. I was suicidal for two years. People would ask, "Hey, how are you?" My response was typically something like, "I'm great. Life is great, and I have a lot of friends. I go hiking a lot. I'm really happy." Meanwhile, my internal dialogue was more like, "Ughhhh. I'm going to kill myself."

People can't read minds, so they would say, "Okay, great!" And then I would think, "Obviously that person doesn't care about me if they can't tell that I'm lying."

This habit was destructive, and pushed me further into isolation and shame. My behavior reflected the thoughts I was *assuming*, it was not based on the reality of the present moment. It is not another person's job to figure out when you truly desperately need help. Only you can do that.

If others could read my mind, they would know:

1.

2.

3.

EXAMPLES:
- I had a terrible nightmare last night
- I think I'm getting depressed.

NEXT COOL THING YOU COULD DO:
share these things with a supportive friend, family member, or therapist.

I used to think I needed to wait six months or up to a year before alerting the troops that I was depressed. I thought alerting anyone sooner would be crying wolf.

"What if this fogginess only lasts one day?" I'd ask. Or think later, "I talked to all of these people and wasted their time because it was just a down day and not actually the beginning of a terrible time." It was so hard to get to a place where I could say, "You know, I'm feeling a bit foggy and depressed today," without being worried that people would think I am a rollercoaster.

I am no longer afraid to let people know when I feel like shit, even when it *is* just for an hour. I eventually realized that the stress I was experiencing was completely preventable. All I needed to do was overcome my biggest fear: tell someone I am in a place of weirdness.

Accepting that other people cannot read my mind was a huge step forward. It helped me see that if I am struggling, the best person to swoop in and save the day is me. I have the ability to speak to people about what is really going on.

I am okay with being in a shitty place now and then. Sometimes I get too overwhelmed and it is difficult. However, for the most part, I am able to speak my struggles out loud. I have been able to pick up a vocabulary that helps me articulate my feelings in a rational way (that's the goal, anyway).

It is important to communicate your feelings and needs explicitly. Implying or hinting at what you need won't be effective for very long because things are bound to get mixed up. Communication can be difficult and things can get messy. At least if it's all out there, it's out of you. And if you need help, you can get it, whatever that looks like for you to be healthy.

Forgive Yourself, Admit Mistakes

Sometimes I do stuff that is inconsiderate or blatantly rude, and I just have to own up to that. Most of the time it's unintentional or it's my old manipulation patterns taking hold of me. I am a human being, just like you, who is sometimes shitty to myself and to other people. I learned from many incredible people in many special places that we must admit our wrongs to ourselves and to other people. Part of personal growth means admitting when you are shitty. This is about showing up for yourself and showing up for those around you.

If you do something shitty, you'll frequently feel absolutely terrible and self-conscious about it. So, how can you undo self-loathing? For me, I first work on getting to a place of peace with myself, and then I take a step back to acknowledge what I can with the person whom I am struggling with.

The first step is to eliminate that negative voice in your head. What does that even mean? Address the rude things you tell yourself and balance them with some true and positive self-talk.

To work on self-talk, try coming up with balancing thoughts for *each* of your negative thoughts. If you are thinking that you are terrible at skateboarding, change that thought to, "I am excited to continue getting better at skateboarding."

It's important to come up with a balancing thought that you'll believe in the moment of negative self-talk. It helps to write them down so you can refer to them if you forget in the moment. This is a skill I learned from studying Kristin Neff, a pioneer of self-compassion work.

Here's an example of some balancing thoughts (try coming up with your own, too!)

Once you get to a place of compassion with yourself, you will be able to breathe through the situation and begin to look at your part in the struggle. You can forgive yourself and take responsibility for your actions.

By implementing some positive self-talk, you'll be better able to acknowledge your wrongs without feeling shame. Address the people you have hurt. If pride gets in the way, it's hard to move forward in relationships. Sometimes we just need to have that talk.

Remember that apologizing to someone doesn't mean you'll get an apology in return. That's not what it's about. You need to clear your Self of the negative behaviors that hold you back. Acknowledging these behaviors aloud can help relieve them, and help you move forward.

Our negative actions frequently have consequences that impact others and we feel better in the long run when we take responsibility for them. *Negative consequences for unproductive behaviors are usually a result of avoidance, not evidence of our worthlessness.*

Come up with some balancing thoughts you can use to combat negative self-talk!

NEGATIVE PHRASE	BALANCING THOUGHT
"I will never get this right."	"I learn more each time I do this."
"Nobody cares about me."	"I am unconditionally worthy of love."

Take Responsibility

WHO DO YOU NEED TO APOLOGIZE TO?

WHAT HAPPENED?

WHAT UNPRODUCTIVE BEHAVIOR(s) DID YOU ACT ON?
(impulsivity, anger, verbal abuse, manipulation, etc.)

WHAT IS SOMETHING DIFFERENT YOU COULD DO
IN FUTURE SITUATIONS?

SUPER SORRY

WHAT ARE YOU APOLOGIZING FOR?
Be specific...

WHAT LESSONS ARE YOU LOOKING FOR?

WHAT CAN YOU SEE HERE? IS THIS PART OF A PATTERN?

WHAT POSITIVE BEHAVIOR WILL YOU PRACTICE INTENTIONALLY?

TRYING NEW STUFF

COMMUNICATE, COLLABORATE, HEAL, AND LEARN

Why would a new behavior be helpful?

What would your life look like if you let go of old patterns?

Who offers valuable guidance?

TRY NEW STUFF

FILL IN THE BLANKS:

When I _____, I will
(EXPERIENCE TRIGGER)

_____

(NEW & REALISTIC & FULFILLING BEHAVIOR)

SORRY, COLLABORATE AND LISTEN

· HOW COULD THIS TEACH YOU TO BE PURPOSEFULLY KIND?
  (How are you going to be less shitty now?)

  → HOW ARE YOU SHEDDING YOUR EGO?

· WHAT CAN YOU TELL YOUR BRAIN WHILE HEARING THE KIND OF FEEDBACK THAT SUCKS TO HEAR?

  → This self-compassionate phrase: _____

  → I am inhaling. I am exhaling. I am learning.

  → I must allow those I love to express their true selves.

  →

  →

REPLACE THE WORD "BUT" WITH THE WORD "AND." FOR EXAMPLE:

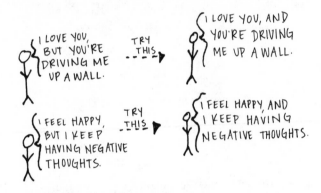

Using the word "but" seems to discredit or push aside what was said before. By saying "and" instead, you are creating space for both statements to be true and acknowledged.

Enjoy Movement

WHAT ARE THREE SONGS THAT REALLY
   GET YOUR BONES GROOVIN' AND GET
   YOU MOVIN'?

1.

2.

3.

FOUR: SAY, "THANK YOU"

In the midst of shitty types of weirdness,
it's easy and natural to lose touch with
any feelings of gratitude.

Try inviting some gratitude to this moment.
Find something in your surroundings that
you are grateful for.

focus your attention on that one
thing.

ONE THING YOU SEE

Once you have eyes on one thing you're grateful for, you can bring more attention to feelings of gratitude.

Describe the characteristics of this object.
- COLORS
- TEXTURE
- SMELL
- WEIGHT
- SIZE
- MATERIALS
- PLACEMENT
- TINY DETAILS
- _____

With each category, release tension in your body and take deep, grateful breaths.

THERE IS SO MUCH TO BE GRATEFUL FOR.

I FEEL KINDA GRATEFUL. I'M STILL PISSED THOUGH.

YOU CAN FEEL BOTH.

Gratitude Lists

A wonderful way to start a gratitude practice is by making a gratitude list everyday. I used to make a twenty-five-item gratitude list every morning. Now I make a five-item gratitude list and I spend more time soaking in the gratitude I feel for each thing I put on that list.

You can choose any number you want from one to one million. You don't need to put pressure on yourself to come up with something really profound to be grateful for. One of the things I am most grateful for right now is that I paid my bills and still had money left over to buy a nice new pen. I can think about all of that and feel that gratitude.

Gratitude lists are great to implement in your daily life. Then, when shit really gets you down, you can keep practicing them. If you're in such a dark place that you can't think of anything good and you can't feel grateful, that's okay. You don't need to beat yourself up because you can't think of anything good about your day or even anything good about your life. Instead, you can look back at old gratitude lists and old happy things and try to feel hope that you will get through the storm.

When you are acknowledging what you are grateful for, be sure to really take time and study your gratitude for this thing. If you are thinking of a person, imagine giving that person a hug. If you are thinking of an object, study it in your head and feel the gratitude in your heart. Gratitude is not just about naming everything you see. It is about keeping a mindful focus on the way your gratitude for this particular thing feels.

This shit changes your brain.

WHAT ARE YOU GRATEFUL FOR?
TRY THIS EVERYDAY!

1.

2.

3.

4.

5.

TIPS!

- see each thing you're grateful for vividly in your mind.
- Take a long inhale and thank it for existing.
- Recall your favorite memory with each item on your list.
- When you put a person on your gratitude list, let them know! It will make your friendship smile.
- write sentimental (or not!) thank you cards.

Thank Others

Gratitude requires conscious acknowledgement of the things and people in your life that bring you joy, lessons, or awareness. You can bring your gratitude to life by taking a pause and diving into the details of the way your heart feels when you think lovingly of someone—then you can say, "Thank you."

You can thank someone for no reason other than you thought of them and felt uplifted. There is no need to wait until a friend does something especially nice for you. Their existence is enough reason to say thank you.

One of my love languages is words of affirmation, and it is one of my favorite ways to express my gratitude. It might have something to do with the fact that I'm always worried about people, so I just need them to know that I love them. It makes me really appreciate people, and need to say it. If there is someone you care about, do something for them that makes them feel heard. Maybe you could run to the grocery store for them, or do their dishes, or give them a big hug.

If there are people in your life who have made a positive impact on your growth, take time to feel that in your heart and to pass on that love. Say, "Hey, thank you. Even in the smallest ways, you have changed my life." If there are people who make you feel that, tell them about it; it's a very cool thing to hear. These moments of sharing create an even stronger sense of connection and positivity. They grow your friendship. You are important to each other, and you know it.

EXPRESS YOUR GRATITUDE!
(TO YOUR HUMANS)

LIST 3 PEOPLE YOU'RE GRATEFUL FOR:

1.

2.

3.

PICK ONE (OR ALL) OF THOSE PEOPLE AND WRITE
THREE THINGS YOU APPRECIATE ABOUT THEM

1._____   2._____   3._____

  A.   A.   A.

  B.   B.   B.

  C.   C.   C.

THINK ABOUT THIS SLOWLY, LET YOUR SHOULDERS
RELAX INTO YOUR GRATITUDE.

LET YOURSELF ACKNOWLEDGE HOW COOL IT IS THAT
THESE PEOPLE EXIST.

EXISTENCE IS WEIRD. NICE HUMANS MAKE IT
WEIRD IN A GOOD WAY.

SAY, "HEY, IF YOU'VE EVER WANTED TO DIE, I'M
REALLY GLAD YOU DIDN'T."

Happy Jars

My favorite thing about January 1st of each new year has become making my first entry in my happy jar. In 2013, a friend told me about this and I totally loved and embraced it. It seemed like a challenge, and one that I could take on.

A happy jar is not hard to make. You can get any jar and any piece of paper. I use a mason jar and index cards. On the outside, write "daily happy things." At the end of every day, sit down and write the date and one thing that you liked about the day on a scrap of paper.

Sometimes, you won't be able to come up with anything good. Maybe you had a bad day, lost a loved one, or just feel too depressed. On days when you really struggle, stick with "I inhaled oxygen." Then try to take a deep breath and just connect to the present for just a moment, even if it's difficult.

On particularly wonderful days, it may be difficult to come up with only one thing. The temptation to summarize the entire day arises. This part is awesome because then you can hyper-focus on the super good day and scroll through all of the awesome moments to find the one you want to write.

Both of these difficulties are actually quite nice. You either have to think of something good and embrace positivity for just moment, or you get to bask in the goodness of a wonderful day.

An added bonus to this practice is that throughout the day you might remember, "Oh, I have to find something to put in my happy jar tonight," and start looking for good stuff. Guess what happens when you look for good stuff? You see a lot more good stuff.

Each year, I start a new happy jar. Now that it has been a few years, I have a row of happy jars from previous years. I get to go back whenever I want and pick a nice thing from a jar so that I can look back at a really nice moment.

HAPPY JARS!

1. FIND AN EMPTY JAR

2. PUT THE DATE ON A SMALL PIECE OF PAPER

3. ON THE SAME PIECE OF PAPER, WRITE YOUR FAVORITE THING FROM THE DAY

4. PUT THAT PIECE OF PAPER IN THE JAR

NOW YOU HAVE ONE MORE PIECE OF EVIDENCE THAT LIFE IS COOL.

FOR NOW, ANSWER THESE:

1. What was your favorite thing about yesterday?

2. What are you looking forward to today?

FIVE: TAKE A SHOWER

YOU'RE DOING A GREAT JOB. YOU'RE DOING STUFF TO HELP CURRENT YOU AND FUTURE YOU AND EVEN PAST YOU.

Here's another thing you could do: take a shower!

Showers are awesome because at some point in the routine, you'll notice, "oh, yeah, I'm in the shower." And that's exactly what present moment awareness is.

SO FRESH

- Go heavy on your nice smelling body wash.
  - if you don't have any, that's okay
- Focus on your breath and on how the water feels.
- Clean your bellybutton, wash your toes, let go of the darkness you are able to at this point.

- Moisturize
- Put on any clothes you want

Practice Daily (Future You Will Thank You)

Coping skills are sort of like brushing your teeth. You wake up in the morning, and you brush your teeth. It's not a big to-do, it's not something you only do every couple of months. Even on difficult and weird days, I mostly wake up and brush my teeth. Even on the mornings of funerals. That day is hard, but I don't grapple a terrible amount with whether or not I should brush my teeth (There are exceptions to this, and you get the idea).

You should approach coping skills the same way most people approach brushing their teeth. Normal. Something we do everyday. You can better prepare yourself for future difficulties by practicing coping skills now.

Practicing the skills in this book is awesome at any time. Practicing them when things are consistent is a great way to get really comfortable. Even if you aren't struggling, you can experiment and see what works for you. Then, when dark days happen, it's much easier to practice the skills that assist in getting through the sludge.

A mindfulness activity a day is just part of it. Five mindful minutes of organizing buttons or observing the sky, or *even* brushing your teeth. Two minutes to write yourself a self-compassion note or make a gratitude list. Thirty minutes at the gym. A yoga class. Taking the dog on a walk. Listening to a short meditation on YouTube during a work break.

Think of every stressful or emotional situation as recon. You go into it and you react in whatever way you react. Afterward, look at the situation and observe your part in it and where you could have expressed your Self in a more effective way. Then, decide to try something new the next time you are in that stressful situation, such as a coping or communication skill, and see if that works or not.

Every moment is a lesson. Approach life that way to inspire your curiosity.

Show Up

When I used to get depressed, I had no idea what to do with myself. It felt like there was no hope of escape. All I could do was lay in bed and try as hard as I could to go back to sleep. I didn't know how to slow my thoughts down. I didn't know how to coax myself out of my bed.

Now I have only one thing I try to do when I get so depressed—I "show up." When you are depressed, show up to the very best of your ability; not emotionally, not mentally, but physically.

Show up to the grocery store to buy your dogs their dog food. Show up to your work to the very best of your ability. Even if you can't find words to say, even if you can't leave your house, do your very best to at least get out of bed. Once you're out of bed, the hardest battle is won. Some days, you can't get out of bed. That's okay.

If you're able to make your bed, you can feel even better. When you take a shower, focus on the warm water and the smell of your body wash. Notice if you are starting to feel better. "Better" for a massively depressed person, anyway.

When you're not depressed, you can still make your bed and shower: habits that are great to practice when things are fine, so they're just a bit easier when things are shitty. Or they don't seem so impossible or uncomfortable, because you're used to doing them.

Some days gravity suctions me to my bed and disappointment colors all of my thoughts. Taking action can be so hard, I used to think I could only do anything if I was not in a bout of depression. I felt like I was being crushed by this darkness. How can I walk and breathe and talk with this huge weight hindering every moment and everything I do?

Some days, I feel hidden in the shadows of my thoughts and the corners of my brain that tell me, "This is how it will always be: terrible, failing, frustrating."

I pull myself out of these black holes of seemingless constant depression by shining the light on the shadows. I shine the light primarily by talking about it and being grateful, and *showing up*.

I let people know, "This is where my mind is today." And they love me anyway. Love is my connection to reality. Love from others, love from myself. So as much as I can, when I can, I show up for it.

BRAINSTORM WAYS THAT YOU CAN SHOW UP FOR YOUR LIFE & LOVED ONES. (CIRCLE THE ONES YOU LIKE! ADD YOUR OWN!)

Call someone to be on the phone while you get out of bed.

take a shower

go on a walk if you're feeling stuck.

take notes of things to remember if your memory sucks

encourage your friends as they grow & learn

Think ten minutes at a time

take a dance break (if you don't want to dance, play a song and daydream about your amazing dance moves)

1.

2.

3.

Aim for Consistency, Not Certainty

I set out to write this chapter about how it is okay to live an ordinary life. I wanted to explain that it's okay to *not* travel the world and go on all sorts of adventures. I thought that by having a few friends and a steady day job I was living an ordinary life. Thinking of my life as "ordinary" felt comfortable.

What I learned is that there is no such thing as an ordinary life. I thought *ordinary* was boring and I thought boring sounded good. Let me tell you something, ordinary is not very boring. It's really all about consistency, because nothing is 100% chill all the time. If you have things you wake up and do every day, they can help tether you to some comfort in the chaos.

There might be an ordinary day, or an ordinary couple of months. Things happen, and hearts break and fill and break again. Some things are so big, and change so much, that they are nothing like ordinary. Hearts always fill again.

Through it all, the goal is consistency. Not certainty. Consistency looks like a daily routine that is structured around self-care. No matter what bullshit life brings, you still wake up, make your bed, brush your teeth, write a gratitude list. Building habits that you do everyday will help in times of intense *un*certainty.

The desire for consistency does not mean that my expectation is to make things never uneasy again. I perform my daily routines

EVERY DAY

WHAT SIMPLE TASKS HELP YOU PAUSE?
(CIRCLE SOME! ADD YOUR OWN!)

Doing the dishes

drinking water

1.

2.

cleaning

3.

folding clothes

organizing the bookshelf

TRY INCORPORATING THESE THROUGHOUT YOUR DAY IN A WAY THAT IS REALISTIC AND SUSTAINABLE!

in order to bring me back to the moment. Everyday, I brush my teeth. Today sucks, I'm still going to brush my teeth. Consistency is ordinary, and ordinary can be fun to explore.

Like so many of these tools, I see this as something that enhances every single day. These skills are not just there for when the dark days come. They help me stay in and soak up the present moment, even if it's just for a moment.

Start thinking about the things that you would like to do every day to take care of yourself and establish a healthy routine.

WHAT WOULD YOU LIKE TO ADD TO YOUR DAY?

Imagine what your life would look like if you practiced gratitude and self-compassion naturally, as a part of your morning and evening routines. In the space below, brainstorm what you might want to include in your daily habits.

MORNING: _____

NIGHT: _____

A FEW IDEAS TO GET YOU STARTED:
· SAY "I LOVE YOU" IN THE MIRROR   · GRATITUDE LIST
· JOURNAL FOR 20 MINUTES   · MEDITATE
· TAKE 10 MINDFUL BREATHS
· MAKE THE BED

ROUTINE CHECK

CURRENT

MORNING
- First five things you do in the morning

1.

2.

3.

4.

5.

EVENING
- Last five things you do before sleep.

1.

2.

3.

4.

5.

- CROSS OFF WHAT YOU'LL REMOVE FROM YOUR ROUTINE

WHAT TO ADD

CIRCLE (& ADD YOUR OWN)
- ACTIONS YOU'D LIKE IN YOUR ROUTINE.

gratitude list

clean the kitchen

shower

journal

drink 1 glass of water

walk the dog

jumping jacks

meditate

read

NEW

WHAT IS YOUR IDEAL ROUTINE?

THINGS THAT MAKE
LIFE COOLER

CIRCLE WHAT YOU WANT
ADD YOUR OWN

DANCE
BREAKS

therapy

MEDS

positive
affirmations

A CONSISTENT
ROUTINE

FUN EXERCISE
HABITS

books that
inspire growth

ENERGY
HEALING

emotional
intelligence

easy
party
themes

QUIET
THINKING
TIME

some kind of
spiritual practice

85

Six: Say, "I Love You"

Hey, I'm really proud of you. It takes courage, humility, self-awareness, and effort to take positive action. Especially when everything sucks.

I really care about you. I encourage you now to give yourself true, gentle, and caring attention.

The experiences that have hardened you do not have to keep you from being gentle. You are allowed to be sweet to yourself by acknowleding that you need loving tenderness.

COURAGEOUS SELF-LOVE

YOU CAN ADMIT YOUR NEED FOR TENDERNESS.
COMFORT YOURSELF WITH UNCONDITIONAL SWEETNESS.

try saying this to yourself—

- "I give you permission to need love."

- "I am proud of you for exactly who you are. There is nothing wrong with you."

- "I am learning to love you. Nothing needs to change in order for you to be fully loved."

Also—

If this is uncomfortable, you're totally on the right track. If you're cool with it, I suggest you keep this going daily. It's really helped me. Obviously if you hate this, you can forget it.

Be Kind to Yourself First

You are a small being with a huge heart and you truly *are doing your best.* Even when you feel trapped in bed all day, you are doing your best. So, be kind to yourself. Connect with others authentically and treat yourself to truth and peace. Take a bath. Watch your favorite movie.

You are living life every day with no roadmap or idea of the future. That sucks. It's scary.

It's okay. Be kind to yourself.

Let's say you have a job interview tomorrow. You're preparing. Imagining. You think you're going to get the job. You're afraid you're going to get the job. What if you don't? What if it goes terribly? What if you're not enough?

And then you go, and the interview is great, and you do get the job. Or, you go, and the interview is great, and you don't get the job. Or, you go, and you make a fool of yourself and you are shamed until the next decade. Anything can happen.

Be kind to yourself, you cannot tell the future. Look in the mirror and say, "I love you." Do that every day, for thirty days.

You are here right now. That's just the way it unfolded. The fact that you are here is really important. You are here, you need to learn and open up as much as you can. Lessons only move forward if you let them grow.

BE INTENTIONALLY KIND

LIST 10 THINGS YOU COULD DO IN YOUR DAILY LIFE TO BE KIND TO OTHERS.

1.
2.
3.
4.
5.
6.
7.
8.
9.
10.

LIST 10 THINGS YOU COULD DO IN YOUR DAILY LIFE TO BE KIND TO YOURSELF

1.
2.
3.
4.
5.
6.
7.
8.
9.
10.

Ultimately, this isn't about you. It's not about anyone, really. You're an atom in a living organism. You don't have a say about what that huge living organism does. What you do have a say in is its health. And its overall health determines what it does.

You can do and be whatever you want. You can be a computer programmer. You can value luxury and buy cars. You can work at a non-profit organization. You can drive the city bus or sing for stadiums full of people. You can do all of those things at the same time. Whatever the fuck there is to do, you can do that.

Being kind also happens to feel really, really good. When you open yourself up, you are allowing love, vulnerability, connection. Give that gift to yourself. You deserve it. Feel good.

You matter, your ego does not. You are here and you need love in order to give love. You deserve love. Others deserve love. Love feels good. You don't need to shy away from that anymore.

As a part of the world we live in, there are social contracts we have to follow. That does not have to be as restricting as it sometimes feels. Meditate. Stretch. Breathe. Be kind.

Nothing matters, be kind.

Take care of Your Inner Child

We all have remnants of the small child we were and always will be, who just wants love and acceptance. It can be hard to get that from our parents all of the time, for our whole lives. They are humans, they get annoyed, too.

Perhaps you felt conditional love. I did. I felt loved off and on throughout my childhood, and I have found myself seeking acceptance *still*. This led me to my inner-child practice.

There's a cool concept, called regression, that deals with how small things our parents and loved ones do can trigger behavior and feelings that are left over from *forever* ago. You might hear a certain tone of sigh from your dad and feel like a five-year-old again. Instantly sucked back to feelings of fear.

The thing that might be stopping you from feeling good is that you might not be *connected* to your inner child. I know this might sound weird, okay? Bear with me. It's some of the coolest work I have done.

I added inner child work to my healing practices and I felt instantly in my element. When I looked at baby pictures of myself, I totally empathized with what that child felt. I looked with a compassionate lens and I felt a lot of emotion for what that tiny kid was going through.

Slowly and surely, I have noticed changes in myself and in my relationships. Because I have begun to take over as my own loving parent, I don't need to rely so much on others to give me permission to feel secure, loved, held, or anything else 5-year-old Sim did not always feel. I can give her those things in every moment by opening up a dialogue with that part of me that still exists.

Before going into a stressful or scary situation (such as a serious talk or a budget meeting), talk to your inner child. Say, "Hey sweet kid, you can relax and let me take care of whatever comes next. You do not need to worry, I will keep you safe."

For example, I was walking into a business meeting that seemed intimidating. I checked in with my inner five-year-old to see what she was feeling. She was afraid she wouldn't be heard, that she'd be looked over. These fears were making her feel small already. That manifests as me speaking quietly or not making eye contact with my colleagues. That is not an authentic expression of what a badass I am. I'm here to be heard. I am worthy of being heard.

So, I tell little Sim, "Hey, you are safe, sweet girl. This meeting will be productive and helpful. I will be mindful and assertive, so you do not have to worry. Grown-up Sim is going to do this one." And then I might do a power pose or say a positive affirmation in the mirror. As I do this, I find myself with better posture, clearer ideas, really feeling into my power.

Inner child work is all about owning your power while acknowledging that much of your fear and strife comes from things you got or didn't get at certain ages. By connecting with those phases of my life, you are able to see what behavior stems from what age, and what need that age may represent. And then you get to fill up your own heart with all of the love you could ever need.

You can get connected to your inner child by pulling up an old photo of yourself at any age that you feel called to. Look at that photo. Think about that child and consider their mannerisms and needs. See that photo and that child as a different person from you who you know very well. In that moment, what did that child need that they were not getting? What was that child happy about?

You might notice that you will feel a stronger connection with some ages more than others. That's why I talk about my inner-five-year-old so much. I totally feel connected with that scared and silly little girl.

As you become your own loving parent, when you feel the need to get comfort or love, give it to yourself. Get quiet and think, "What does my [fill in the blank: five-year-old, seventeen-year-old] self need to feel safe and loved right now?"

You can begin to explore different things that make your inner child feel acknowledged. Doing this practice over time will help you be more compassionate to yourself. When you feel mixed up and overwhelmed, take a moment to pause. Is this coming from another part of you that needs some expectations met?

Now I see the inner child in many people. I can connect with that. I can be compassionate to people who piss me off because I know that they are in the same world as I am. We are children and we are learning how to do life.

- LOOK IN THE MIRROR. SAY, "I WILL TAKE CARE OF YOU."
- DO THE BEST YOU CAN TO DO THE BEST YOU CAN. IT IS OKAY
  YOUR BEST TODAY IS LESS MAGNIFICENT THAN YESTERD
- LISTEN TO YOUR FAVORITE SONG FROM 10 YEARS AGO
- MAKE A LIST OF MOMENTS IN YOUR LIFE WHEN YOU FELT P
  OF YOURSELF (EVEN IF THEY'RE LESS IMPRESSIVE LOOKING BACK)
- PUT ON YOUR FAVORITE OUTFIT   · LEARN TO COOK
- LEARN TO GROCERY SHOP   · EAT EVERY 3-5 HOURS
- MAKE THE DECISION THAT IS BEST FOR YOU   · VOTE
- READ/LISTEN TO **BE KIND TO** · ASK YOUR
  BOOKS YOU LOVE   FRIEND F
- GIVE YOUR   A HUG
  FRIEND A HUG   **YOURSELF**   · GO TO TH
- SPEND ONE WHOLE   DENTIST
  HOUR SPEAKING   · GIVE YOURSELF
  KINDLY TO YOURSELF   A HUG
- LOOK AT YOUR BODY LOVINGLY. SAY, "HEY, BODY, THANK YOU."
- GO TO THERAPY   · ACKNOWLEDGE ALL OF YOUR FEELINGS
- PET YOUR ANIMAL AND RELIVE YOUR HAPPY MEMORIES
- HANG OUT WITH PEOPLE YOU WANT TO BE LIKE
- READ YOUR FAVORITE CHILDREN'S BOOK
- SHOW OFF YOUR DANCE MOVES   · TELL THE TRUTH
- EXPLORE WHAT BRINGS YOU COMFORT IN UNCERTAINTY
- TAKE RESPONSIBILITY FOR YOUR BEHAVIOR, SEE IF THERE
  IS A LESSON YOU COULD LEARN
- LET GO OF RELATIONSHIPS THAT HURT YOUR FEELINGS
- LOOK AT YOUR BABY PHOTOS. SAY, "I WILL TAKE CARE OF YOU."
- STAND WITH YOUR BAREFEET ON THE GROUND FOR 10 MINUTE
- PUT ON SOCKS AND SLIDE ACROSS THE ROOM
- PLAY AN INSTRUMENT

- USE SPECIFIC LANGUAGE TO TELL YOUR FRIEND YOU APPRECIATE THEM
- REMEMBER NAMES. IF YOU FORGET, ASK AGAIN
- ASK, "WHAT ARE YOU PARTICULARLY GRATEFUL FOR TODAY?"
- GIVE OR RECOMMEND BOOKS TO YOUR FRIENDS
- LET THE CAR IN FRONT OF YOU GET OVER · DRAW A PICTURE
- LEAVE A NICE NOTE ON THE RECEIPT FOR YOUR SERVER
- LET THE SQUIRREL CROSS THE STREET
- GO TO YOUR FRIEND'S ART SHOW   · WRITE A NOTE
- SAY, "HEY, WHERE ARE THE REST OF OUR FRIENDS? CAN WE INVITE THEM?" WHEN YOU NOTICE PEOPLE BEING LEFT OUT.
- PICK UP TRASH
- READ YOUR FRIEND'S BLOG
- LISTEN TO YOUR FRIEND WHEN THEY SHARE TRUTH

BE KIND TO OTHERS

- MAKE DINNER
- VOTE
- LISTEN
- SMILE & MAKE EYE CONTACT (WHEN SAFE & APPROPRIATE)

- VOLUNTEER SOMEWHERE THAT WILL HELP YOU GET TO KNOW PEOPLE YOU MAY NOT OTHERWISE MEET. LISTEN.
- SAY, "WHAT CAN I DO TO HELP YOU CONQUER THIS FEAR?"
- OPEN THE DOOR AND SAY, "HELLO" (IF YOU WANT) WITH A SMILE
- INTRODUCE YOURSELF TO YOUR NEIGHBORS
- LET PEOPLE KNOW THAT YOU SEE THEM
- LET PEOPLE KNOW THAT YOU HEAR THEM
- LET GO OF CONTROL
- DONATE YOUR CLOTHES WHEN YOU CLEAR YOUR CLOSET
- DONATE YOUR MONEY IF YOU CAN
- REMEMBER THAT IF YOU THINK YOUR FRIEND'S HOBBY IS DUMB, IT DOESN'T MAKE YOUR FRIEND OR THEIR HOBBY DUMB.
- HELP PEOPLE FIND ANSWERS BY HELPING THEM GET TO THE RESOURCES THEY NEED.

SEVEN: WRITE

IT COULD HELP TO GET YOUR THOUGHTS FROM BRAIN TO PAPER. CLEAR OUT THOSE COBWEBS OF CHAOTIC THOUGHT.

What are you holding on to? Is there a moment/facial expression/phrase you are stuck on?

How would you feel and behave if you could magically let go with total peace?

THOUGHTS & FEELINGS

CIRCLE AT LEAST 3 FEELING WORDS.
WHERE DO THESE FEELINGS COME FROM?
CAN YOU RELEASE THEM?

grateful angry fearful happy
content confused ashamed
optimistic anxious irritable loved
sad curious excited hurt ignored
willing relaxed compassionate enthusiastic
heartbroken disappointed skeptical
hopeless hopeful confident

REMEMBER

- YOUR THOUGHTS ARE NOT FACTS. They do not need to dictate your feelings.
- THE FEELINGS YOU'RE EXPERIENCING IN THIS MOMENT do not need to dictate your behavior.

Write It out

The state of our country, and world, often gets me incredibly sad. I find myself slipping into a serious state of pessimism and doubt. Hope I once had vanishes and I am left feeling angry. Existential angst... What is this shit all about?

When I am in these states of bewilderment and fear, I write about it. A lot.

I keep a journal that I write in every morning. I write about my day, I write about yesterday, I write reviews about the type of pen I am using. Usually this helps me get out all of my jumbled thoughts in a stream-of-consciousness release. Sometimes I can come to conclusions and better understanding of the fear and doubt I have. I can find the source of that fear, where it comes from and how I can embrace something positive instead.

It took time and practice to get to a place where I could actually cope with depression in a healthy way. In no way am I a master of depression. I know new things about it now.

I was never totally sure if the depression would end. Every time I got depressed, for years, I was convinced that it would never end. Depression cycles through my life, and I forget the fact that it is a cycle as soon as I'm depressed. To help me remember, I have this reminder written on a flashcard on the wall in my bedroom:

depression is never forever, my dear.

Often times I write about these concepts that affect me, and I come to an even broader understanding of the situations and my place in them. Whether the situation is my ended marriage or a stubbed toe, writing about it helps me separate my emotions from my core. They're on paper now. I can breathe better now. Maybe, I can talk about them now.

In talking about my feelings of emptiness, fear, and confusion, I am able to feel a relief that does not solve anything, it simply helps me come to a better place of acceptance. Acceptance doesn't mean I get to a place where I am cool with everything. It means I accept the present moment and choose which action I want to take next.

By writing things out, and reminding yourself that you are okay when you are in this moment (even if you don't believe that yet), you will lift your own spirits, you might feel a sense of relief. If you get emotional while you are writing, end your flow with a positive affirmation or intention for the day.

Pros and Cons

Something I learned from my therapists was the value of making two pros and cons lists for a decision. One of the lists could be pros and cons about "why I should…" eat pizza, for example, the second one could be the pros and cons of "why I shouldn't…" eat pizza. I'd also like to note that you can eat as much pizza as you want, whenever you want. This is just an example.

You might think that those two lists will turn out exactly the same. There will be some overlap, and you might find that you get a bigger picture of the decision you want to make.

PIZZA PROS & CONS

ORDER PIZZA

PROS	CONS
· Pizza is delicious	· Heartburn
· I don't know what to eat	· Not healthy
· Leftovers	· I already have other food at home
· I have a coupon	

DON'T ORDER PIZZA

PROS	CONS
· Learn to cook	· Inconvenient to cook
· Save money	· No leftovers
· Groceries won't go bad	· Told my roommate it's pizza night

PROS & CONS TEMPLATE

USE THIS TEMPLATE TO GET A WELL-ROUNDED
VIEW OF A DECISION YOU ARE FACING.

PROS & CONS OF YES ↓

PROS	CONS

PROS & CONS OF NO ↓

PROS	CONS

Address Grief

Grief is hard. I can't even hear the word without thinking of some very special people that I have lost, and some of the biggest of the trials I have faced. Especially as I have grappled with the concept of my own mortality for so many years.

We all struggle with grief in different ways, and every way is okay. It's about allowing the pain to flow through you and out of you.

When one of my dear friends committed suicide, I was shaken to the core. I still am. I wrote him a lot of letters in the beginning. I still write him letters sometimes. It helps me feel closer and connected. It helps me honor the person I love and miss dearly. I get to acknowledge it by expressing myself in writing and taking myself to the place where I am with them.

Try writing a letter to a source of your pain, such as a lost loved one. Thank them for everything you learned from them, the joy or comfort they made you feel, or the effects they had on your life. Be literal or metaphorical. Get creative. If it's hard, take your time.

When I am missing my lost friendships and relationships, I just do my best to give them respect and to honor them. When a major life event happened, I got a small box and put a few things in it that symbolized that time in my life. I lit a candle next to it and wrote a note that said, "I am honoring this while continuing my spiritual growth."

thank you

Stars,

Thank you for being here, even when I cannot see you. Even when I don't look up. Even when I forget you exist.

Thank you for sometimes falling. It reminds me that it's okay to fall. It's beautiful to fall. Falling is even something I can wish upon.

love, Simone

That is one thing that has helped me move forward. I can hold this grief as separate from me, while still acknowledging and honoring it.

You can write anyone you are grieving over a letter. It can be as long or as short as you want. Try to make it at least five sentences, and it's okay if it's shorter than that. Take a moment to address the note to the person you are thinking of and smile at the thought of them. Think of a nice moment or a memory of them that calms you. Think of it as a thank you note. You can address your love and longing for a hug or a laugh. You can even express anger, if you need to.

It's okay to be angry at the people our souls are missing. When you feel you are done with the letter, sign it however you want to and take three deep breaths to transition yourself out of that zone, which can sometimes be intense. You can always take a break if you need to.

A MOMENT TO HONOR YOUR GRIEF & GROWTH

HOLD A PERSON IN YOUR HEART. MAYBE THEY ARE NO LONGER LIVING. MAYBE YOU HAVE LOST THEIR CONNECTION. MAYBE YOU NEED TO LET THEM GO. OPEN YOUR HEART TO COMPASSION AND GRATITUDE. WRITE THEM A NOTE OF APPRECIATION:

Write Yourself a Letter

I f I trace this book to its very birthplace, it was a conversation I had with an amazing woman I would grow to know very well. Near the end of my stay at the psychiatric hospital, we had a conversation where she said, "If you're going to move forward, we need you to be sure that you do not want to kill yourself. How are you going to handle it when you face future hardship?" I bounced around some ideas about the coping skills I had learned and the friends I had made. Somewhere in the conversation she suggested that I write myself a letter. Not to me at that moment, but to future, depressed, potentially suicidal Simone.

I took her advice and I wrote myself a lengthy letter. I agreed to write it because I wouldn't have believed anything it said if it came from anyone else. In those moments, no one else *gets* it. I had the chance to take a step back and look at the patterns that kept me stuck. I thought of all of the loopholes I frequently come up with. I did my best to address and dispel them.

In the following years, I did face hardship (I still do). I faced heartbreak and I coped with the suicide of a dear friend. And I read the letter I had written to myself during a time of great clarity. It was amazing.

During my last two years of heavy suicidality, I wrote a series of essays defending my right to choose death. The letter I wrote in the psychiatric hospital was much different. It was a call to action. It was a request to get help. The entire letter always came back to one thing: Reach out.

It gives me hope. I also sometimes think it is total bullshit, and in the letter, I predict that I think it will be bullshit. I roll my eyes at it, and I keep reading.

The notebook I wrote that turned into this book was based on that letter. And I have taken bits and pieces of themes in that letter and turned them into notes. Really cute notes.

Now, when my mind is racing quickly and I am having trouble slowing down, one of the things I do is write myself a quick note. Most of mine are in the pages of my planner (to find a few months from now) and on notecards throughout my house.

A LETTER TO FUTURE YOU

WRITE A LETTER TO YOUR FUTURE SELF THAT WILL ENCOURAGE
AND GROUND YOU IN MOMENTS OF SELF-DOUBT OR STRESS. IT'S
A LETTER FOR YOU TO SAY, "HEY, YOU, IT'S YOU FROM THE PAST,
LET ME HELP YOU. I'LL TELL YOU SOME STUFF THAT MIGHT
HELP YOU OUT OF THIS FUNK."

ANSWER THESE QUESTIONS TO HELP YOU GET STARTED

WHAT IS YOUR GO-TO HAPPY SONG? ENCOURAGE FUTURE YOU
TO LISTEN TO IT !

WHAT ARE SOME OF YOUR AWESOME CHARACTER TRAITS THAT
ANGRY/NEGATIVE/SAD YOU WILL BELIEVE AND BE ENCOURAGED BY?

WHAT COPING SKILLS WOULD YOU BE WILLING TO TRY?

WHAT ARE SOME NICE THINGS PEOPLE HAVE SAID TO YOU?
SAY THEM TO FUTURE YOU.

NICE NOTES FROM YOU TO YOU.

WRITE YOURSELF SOME KINDNESS & SELF-COMPASSION

Simone,
Thank you for doing life
LOVE, Simone

Simone,
I want to remind you that you are loved!
LOVE, Simone

TIME TO WRITE

TRY THESE SUGGESTIONS TO HELP YOU GET OUT YOUR FURY. MAYBE YOU'LL WRITE YOUR WAY THROUGH THIS WAVE. (I LIKE USING PEN AND PAPER FOR THIS. TYPING IS GREAT, TOO)

▲ WRITE THIS SITUATION FROM A THIRD PERSON POINT OF VIEW, AS THOUGH YOU SAW THIS ON A TV SHOW.

▲ WRITE THE CONCLUSION OF THIS EVENT. HOW WOULD YOU LIKE THIS TO GO? WHAT HAPPENS NEXT?

▲ WRITE WHAT HAPPENED FROM THE PERSPECTIVE OF ANOTHER PERSON INVOLVED.

▲ SET A TIMER FOR TEN MINUTES AND WRITE A STREAM OF CONSCIOUSNESS BLOB OF THOUGHTS. WRITE YOUR THOUGHTS AS THEY COME UP. NO NEED TO MAKE SENSE.

▲ WRITE AN ANGRY OR SAD OR ANNOYED NOTE ABOUT ALL OF THIS NONSENSE. EXPRESS HOW THIS HAS INCONVENIENCED YOU.

▲ IDENTIFY THREE EMOTIONS YOU ARE FEELING. WRITE A "THINKING OF YOU" NOTE TO EACH OF THEM.

FOR EXAMPLE ▷ "Hey, Sadness. I know this really sucks and you want to feel better. We'll work this out. Soon you'll be in the sun."

ENJOYABLE

JOYFUL · LOVED · HAPPY · BRAVE · AWE
FREE · CONFIDENT · PEACEFUL
HOPEFUL · EAGER
INSPIRED · RELAXED
SAFE · BLISS
CONTENT · EMPOWERED
GRATEFUL · VALUED
SPIRITUALLY CONNECTED
ACCEPTED · HEARD · ECSTATIC
UNDERSTOOD · SILLY · SEEN · OPEN
ENERGIZED · CREATIVE · CURIOUS
· OPTIMISTIC · REFRESHED · LOVING

LESS ENJOYABLE

ANGRY · SAD · DEVASTATED
PANIC · FEARFUL · ANXIOUS
HURT · RAGE · REJECTED
TERRIFIED · LOST
MISUNDERSTOOD
BETRAYED · SHAME
FURIOUS · HOPELESS
HELPLESS · LONELY
DEPRESSED · WORRIED
WORRIED · NEGLECTED
GRIEF · IGNORED
CONFUSED · EXCLUDED
MISERABLE · ANNOYED

feeling Word(s)

"When you validate my truth, I feel seen and loved."

"Thank you for allowing me to exist just as I am."

"I am ready to learn the lessons of this day."

"I am safe."

GRATEFUL

"With each breath, I am reminded that I am here. Exactly where I need to be."

"I feel peace in the midst of uncertainty."

"I know that I am loved." "There is joy in every moment."

"I create meaning in my life every day."

"I need some reassurance that I am loved."

"I did/said something I wish I hadn't. I can't let it go."

"My anger right now is a result of my fear that I am unlovable."

SCARED

"I tried to express myself and I didn't feel accepted."

"It seems like no one can really see me."

"When I don't feel loved, I become convinced that no one loves me."

"I feel insecure in my existence."

"I don't know what I'm doing."

"My life doesn't look the way I want it to."

"I don't know what to do."

"I rarely feel inspired."

LOST

"I just have a feeling that something needs to change."

"I am not connected to my community."

"Am I a total failure?"

"I feel like my life is spinning out of control."

"Nothing I do makes me feel secure."

"I frequently question my purpose. I can't figure it out."

WRITING THROUGH FEELINGS

I am feeling some version of...
LIST APPLICABLE FEELING WORDS

My experience in these feelings is...

WHAT JUDGMENTS ABOUT THIS MOMENT ARE LOUDEST?

WHAT IS YOUR VIEW OF YOURSELF?

WHAT IS YOUR VIEW OF OTHERS?

ARE YOU PHYSICALLY FEELING ANYTHING?

HOW IS YOUR BREATHING?

ARE ∨ THINKING ABOUT THE PAST? PRESENT? FUTURE?
YOU ☺

Use these questions to get you started and
go from there.

EIGHT: THINK ABOUT HOW COOL YOU ARE

HEY, YOU'RE GREAT. I KNOW THIS BECAUSE NO ONE IS 100% TERRIBLE IN THE EYES OF 100% OF PEOPLE. EVERYONE IS CHERISHED BY SOMEONE.

Describe two times in your life when someone expressed appreciation for you.

1.

2.

GIVE FUTURE YOU PERMISSION TO TRULY FEEL LOVED. LET YOURSELF BELIEVE IT.

YOU'RE A COOL PERSON

Make a list of three really cool experiences you've had in your life.

1.

2.

3.

What are four details of personality that you really like?

1.

2.

3.

4.

WHAT WOULD YOU SAY ABOUT YOURSELF IF YOU HAD TOTAL SELF-ACCEPTANCE? YOU'RE ALLOWED TO BELIEVE THAT YOU'RE AWESOME.

Self-Talk and Affirmations

When I go through really dark and scary times, I think about teething babies. Tooth pain sucks. Tooth pain for a baby who has very little experience with pain probably sucks more. At that point in her life, teething is the shittiest thing she's ever gone through. And she makes it through that pain and she goes on to use her teeth for eating delicious food.

You might be in the worst pain you've ever gone through, and it's okay. Every time we go through something new, we are going through it for the first time. Be sweet to yourself the way you'd be sweet to a teething baby. You'll be okay. You are powerful beyond belief. You are precious.

If you looked in the mirror and spoke to yourself with compassion, what would you say? If you are thinking negative thoughts, what can you replace them with? If you don't like the way your life is going, what can you do to become open to opportunity?

One awesome way to increase your self-encouragement is by repeating positive affirmations throughout the day. Louise Hay wrote a book called *You Can Heal Your Life*, and it has changed lives all over the world, including mine. She talks about stopping our negative thought patterns by replacing negative thoughts with positive affirmations.

For example, when I am playing through my cringe reel, Louise Hay suggests saying, "I approve of myself." All day long, say, "I approve of myself, I approve of myself," over and over. Hundreds of times a day, she says. I have done this regularly and it has worked to quell emotional pain about the past. It has become automatic to the point where I say it aloud without noticing sometimes.

There are many resources to find suggestions for positive affirmations. You can google it, you can read books, you can come up with your own. Positive affirmations can change your life if you want them to. Instead of longing for things, we speak as though we already have them. If you are full of self-loathing, you can say, "I love myself unconditionally." If you need something, speak as

You are a human on a mission of goodness. Keep your heart open, come back to your breath.

POSITIVE AFFIRMATIONS

"I love myself more every day"

"I am willing to learn the lessons this moment can teach me."

"I am safe"

"I make a positive impact on the people in my life."

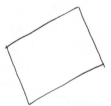

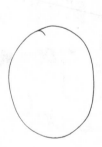

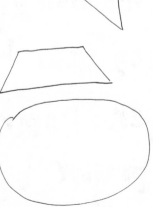

WRITE YOUR OWN!

though you already have it. When you need a new car, say, "I love my new car."

When you expect the positive, it will frequently come. You have the opportunity to change your thinking in its very core, if you want to, by repeating affirmations. When you observe negative thoughts and choose positive ones, you might find yourself feeling resilient and sure of your life.

Say them in the mirror, sing them in the shower, repeat them in your car on your way to work.

In order to come up with your own affirmation, think about what you would believe that could stop your cringe reel, even if just for a moment. What words would you love to hear from your hero? What are the things you most need to hear?

Hey, It's Okay to Not Know

Hello world, my name is Simone DeAngelis and I cooked ground beef for the first time at 24 years old after Googling "how to cook ground beef." I had lived alone for the previous two years on prepared meals, take out, and my dad's cooking. Fried eggs with sriracha was as far as my cooking skills would take me.

I used to think there was a lot more involved in writing a check than is actually involved. Because of this, I avoided writing checks in an attempt to not look like a fool. Finally, at 21 years old, I wrote my first check. Turns out, it's not a task that would typically come up as "challenging."

In third grade I missed the day when we learned how to write a cursive "D." As a result, I still have no idea how to write a cursive "D."

What I'm getting at is that there are things I don't know how to do. Most of these things are possible to learn. If you missed that day, it's okay to ask for a review from a friend or teacher. The first step is to ask a question.

Not knowing how to do something does not mean you are incompetent. It just means you need to ask for help. How can you be expected to do something perfectly, especially on your first attempt?

When I don't know how to do something simple, I say, "I missed that day!" Just like the day I missed the cursive "D," I was also never aware that I should be learning about what the fuck a credit score is. I missed that day, for sure.

Things to Learn

WHAT WOULD YOU LIKE TO LEARN?
   IS THERE INFORMATION YOU ARE CURIOUS ABOUT?
   WHAT TASKS OR ACTIVITIES DO YOU WANT TO TRY?

HOW WOULD YOU LIKE TO LEARN THESE THINGS?
   (TAKE A CLASS, READ A BOOK, ASK A FRIEND,
   TRAVEL, SIGN UP FOR A SPORT, WATCH A VIDEO, ETC.)

WHAT FEARS ARE HOLDING YOU BACK? HOW WILL
YOU TAP INTO YOUR COURAGE AND MOVE FORWARD?

NINE: RELAX

It can be super exhausting to have emotions. You're doing a great job. If you are thinking that you didn't do a great job, try to see it from a different view. You're reading a book about coping with emotions. So, trust me, you're doing a great job.

Give yourself some time to relax. Intentional relaxation is productive and helpful and necessary. If you need the whole day off, take it. Or, give yourself an hour or two.

Free from self-loathing, free from comparison. This about giving the freak out mode you what they need.

INTENTIONALLY CHILL

WHAT CAN YOU GIVE YOURSELF RIGHT NOW to REST? WHAT CAN YOU DO TO EMBRACE A MOMENT THAT IS NOT AT ALL CHAOTIC?

HERE ARE SOME IDEAS

listen to music ○ play an instrument ○ dance
eat (or cook) your favorite meal ○ draw ○ drink tea
throw paint on a canvas ○ go on a walk ○ swim
do a craft project ○ drink tea ○ go on a drive
color in a coloring book ○ hug a comfy blanket
slide across the floor in your socks ○ sing a song
put together a puzzle ○ pet an animal
sit in the grass and look at clouds ○ go surfing

ADD YOUR OWN

When You Need to Scream

Growing up, I saw anger expressed in unpredictable and scary ways. This is true for many of us—we learned to express our emotions by watching our parents. That's what I did. And I did things very similar to them while I was young.

If throwing plates and screaming isn't the answer, what is? You can't just push your anger down or pretend it doesn't exist. Sometimes, saying, "This anger is coming from fear, I do not need to react" just isn't good enough. Sometimes that's bullshit. I don't always believe it. I'm like, "No dude, I'm just fucking pissed. I don't want to deal with fear."

In those moments, I know I am passing a bunch of red flags, and I resort to the notes I have written to myself around my house. Notes from past me, who knows what to do in this situation. I also remember one DBT skill very clearly—"act opposite to emotion." If you want to hurt yourself, go buy yourself flowers instead. If you want to text someone something mean, write them a thank you note that you don't have to give them. This is a great phrase to remember because it helps to at least imagine what you would do if you were taking the positive fork in the road.

That energy has to escape or else it will get all piled up inside and you'll feel like shit. When you just want to scream, do something else. So, what can we do to let that anger go and flow through us?

Things that might help if you're super pissed off

GO ON AN ANGRY RUN

DO A BUNCH OF JUMPING JACKS

VENT TO A TRUSTED FRIEND

WRITE A GRATTITUDE LIST

WRITE AN ANGRY LETTER
(BONUS: WRITE A GENUINELY NICE NOTE TO
THOSE WHO REALLY GRIND YOUR GEARS)

TAKE A NICE BATH

SCREAM IN YOUR CAR

ASK YOUR INNER CHILD: "ARE YOU FEELING MISUNDERSTOOD OR UNLOVED OR SCARED OR ANYTHING? ... HOW CAN I COMFORT YOU NOW?"

brainstorm your own

WHAT TO DO WHEN YOU'RE FEELING ANGRY

INSTEAD OF SENDING THAT IMPULSIVE TEXT, TEXT SOMEONE ELSE ABOUT YOUR SITUATION

INSTEAD OF SAYING THINGS THAT WON'T SERVE THE SITUATION OR RELATIONSHIP, TAKE A PAUSE.

MOVE YOUR BODY, GET THAT ANGRY ENERGY OUT. WHAT WILL YOU DO TO MOVE?
.
.
.

WRITE OUT YOUR ANGER. WRITE A LETTER (NOT TO SEND), WRITE A LONG RANT, WRITE A POEM

WHAT ARE YOUR FAVORITE MINDFULNESS ACTIVITIES?
.
.
.

EASE YOUR ANXIETY

COLOR IN A COLORING BOOK

DO YOGA

ASK FOR HELP

TAKE A DANCE BREAK

inhale for 4 seconds

SQUARE BREATHING

HOLD

HOLD

exhale for 5 seconds

LOOK AT YOUR FAVORITE PICTURES

LOOK AT SOMETHING IN NATURE

PET YOUR DOG OR CAT

MAKE A FLOWER ARRANGEMENT

READ YOUR LETTER TO YOURSELF

WATCH AN EPISODE OF YOUR FAVORITE SHOW

Wanting Happiness

There are moments of clinging and moments of resistance. Buddha taught that all suffering is caused by resistance. We cannot force our desires to come true. When we are trying to manipulate or change things that we cannot predict or control, we're out of ourselves and our truth. Clinging to what we once had, or want right now, will not bring happiness to us. Sitting in that uncomfortability is difficult and crucial for growth.

The truth is, in this moment, you can take a moment to be happy. I learned this Buddhist concept from an incredible woman who was dedicated to guiding me toward peace of mind: In order to be happy, we must let go.

We must let go of our ego. Our ego is judgmental and frequently dissatisfied.

We then let go of all of our wants. We let go of all of those things we think we need to be happy.

All we're left with, when we are here in this moment, is happiness.

HOW TO BE HAPPY

STEP ONE:

WRITE "I want happiness."

STEP TWO:

LET GO OF YOUR EGO

CROSS OUT "I"

"~~I~~ want happiness."

STEP THREE:

LET GO OF ALL THE THINGS YOU THINK YOU NEED

LET GO OF YOUR TIRELESS PURSUIT

CROSS OUT "WANT"

"~~I want~~ happiness."

STEP FOUR:

ALLOW YOURSELF TO FIND HAPPINESS RIGHT HERE

TEN: CONNECT WITH YOUR WORLD

How to CREATE A POSITIVE & AUTHENTIC CONNECTION DURING AN ORDINARY, 1-2 MINUTE ENCOUNTER WITH SOMEONE (AN EASY EXAMPLE IS THE CASHIER AT THE GROCERY).

1. Go to the grocery store. (OR ANYWHERE)

2. Make eye contact with the person in front of you.

3. Ask a casually meaningful question.

IT'S AWKWARD & sometimes weird. Mostly, it is _wonderful_! Try it. IF IT IS NOT COOL, TRY AGAIN WHEN YOU'RE READY.

CASUALLY MEANINGFUL QUESTIONS

"What are you especially grateful for today?"

"What was your favorite moment yesterday?"

"What are you most looking forward to?"

BY ASKING CASUALLY MEANINGFUL QUESTIONS, YOU'LL (MAYBE) FIND THAT YOU'RE MORE CURIOUS & ATTENTIVE WITH HUMANS WHO ARE JUST AS CONFUSED AS YOU PRETEND NOT TO BE.

Be Authentic (Without Shame)

The largest take away I've gained from reading so much Brené Brown is that happy people are authentic. Because, authenticity increases joy. When I first read Brown's *The Gifts of Imperfection*, it really gave a boost to my self-compassion, gratitude, and authenticity practices.

When you can show up in situations as who you really are, you'll feel better overall. When you share yourself with others, you feel bigger, more whole, and connected to your existence in a really peaceful way.

When you feel shame that tells you that you are not worthy, get it out of the dark corners of your mind by *sharing* that shame. By speaking it out loud. I've never had someone tell me, "Wow, what you did was so horrible that you are not worthy of love," even though I have done some things that *still* bring up shame even though I have talked about them. Now the shame doesn't take such a hold on me. And it has less power the more I share it.

One thing I have learned about shame is to be careful who I share it with. I have talked about my shame and my darkness at some really inappropriate times. With the cashier at the grocery store, at work, or when people are having a happy conversation. It's not terrible. I don't regret those times. I just felt weird afterward. That's how I learned that I can avoid those neurotic vulnerability hangovers by being more selective about sharing. I can choose some select people who are close to me to process my shame with when I need to (one of those people is my therapist).

These are intimate pieces that make up the person I am today. I can choose who I show that to, it doesn't mean I am being fake with my barista at the coffee shop. I can show up authentically in public without talking about how much guilt I feel for all the shit I stole when I was a teenager. I don't have to tell people about my trauma in order to qualify as 100% authentic all the time.

Another way to show up authentically is being honest when someone says, "How's your day going?" You can respond by saying, "You know, it's a rough day." You don't need to include that you had a PTSD nightmare the night before or go into detail about why you have PTSD.

the more I practice talking to people, the better I get at talking to people.

YOUR PAIN IS REAL NO MATTER HOW MANY CARS YOU HAVE

I AM SO SAD. LOST. DESPERATE FOR RELIEF. I DON'T KNOW HOW MUCH LONGER I CAN TOLERATE THIS HEARTACHE.

THAT'S DRAMATIC. YOU THINK YOU'RE IN PAIN? THINK OF ALL THE PEOPLE WHO HAVE IT SO MUCH WORSE. YOU HAVE A GOOD LIFE. BE GRATEFUL.

1. I KNOW ABOUT & CARE DEEPLY ABOUT THE SUFFERING OF OTHERS.

2. YEP, MY QUALITY OF LIFE IS VERY GOOD.
   → I CAN BE GRATEFUL & SAD AT THE SAME TIME.

3. I AM IN SO MUCH PAIN, I WANT TO DIE.
   → NO AMOUNT OF PERSPECTIVE WILL CURE MY DARKNESS.

4. I NEED YOU TO TELL ME MY PAIN IS VALID.
   → AND I NEED A HUG.

PAIN IS PAINFUL.

ACKNOWLEDGEMENT ALLOWS HEALING.

REALLY PAINFUL, PAINFULLY REAL

What pain are you feeling that you're ashamed to share with others?

If you could finally vocalize your "smallest" (& often scariest) fears, what response would bring you comfort?

YOU DO NOT NEED TO QUALIFY

INSTEAD OF THIS:

SAY THIS:

THERE ARE NO WORDS FOR THE PAIN I FEEL.

I, TOO, HAVE EXPERIENCED INDESCRIBABLE PAIN. IT WAS HEAVY. THOUGH I DO NOT KNOW YOUR PAIN, I AM HERE TO LOVE & SUPPORT YOU.

OVERSHARING

use these questions to clarify your ideal sharing environments.

DO YOU PREFER SPEAKING OUTDOORS OR INDOORS? IN SMALL SPACES OR LARGE SPACES?

DO YOU NEED TOTAL QUIET OR BACKGROUND NOISE?

HOW DO YOU KNOW WHEN YOU ARE READY TO MOVE ON FROM YOUR STORY?

WHO DO YOU MOST FEEL HEARD BY? WHAT QUALITIES MAKE YOU FEEL HEARD BY THEM? (LOOK for these qualities in future listeners)

IF YOU FEEL YOU HAVE OVERSHARED, SAY, "I am grateful to always learn more about myself."

AN EXAMPLE

BEHAVIOR: More listening, fewer monologues — give my friend's attention

TAKE ONE

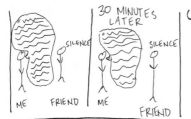

30 MINUTES LATER

SILENCE

ME   FRIEND

SILENCE

ME   FRIEND

6 HOURS AFTER I GET HOME...

OH, I THINK I COULD HAVE LISTENED MORE TODAY. NEXT TIME I WILL TRY SHARING JUST ONE THING INSTEAD OF EVERYTHING.

TAKE TWO

15 MINUTES LATER

3 MINUTES LATER

OH LOOK AT ME GO... IT'S TIME TO LISTEN!

ME   FRIEND

TAKE THREE

I FEEL LOVED WHEN YOU LISTEN. TODAY I WANT TO LISTEN TO YOU!

"I LOVE YOU!"

Live According to Your Values

Values are basically concepts or ideas that contribute to the kind of life you want to live. When you have a stronger understanding of what it actually means to have core values, you are better able to make decisions about your behavior.

When I was first asked to really think about my core values, I didn't know where to start. We did this exercise in psychiatric care where we made a big list of values that we liked. When the big list was done, we had to eliminate five things. We did this over again until there were just 3-5 values left. These were the basis for core values. I currently have five: curiosity, kindness, safety, humor, and purpose. They have mostly stayed the same over the last five-ish years.

And then, the big amazing thing happened. I was asked, "What do these values look like in action?" Though it seems obvious, I had never considered this question. So I did on the next page.

Using my values to make decisions about my day-to-day life has drastically improved the quality of my connections with others, with myself, and with spirituality. I find it absolutely amazing and I can't say enough wonderful things about this practice.

If you want to learn more about this, I encourage you to look into Acceptance and Commitment Therapy (ACT) and how to practice it. There are a lot of really good workbooks out there that can help you implement this stuff in a really simple and realistic way. You can google it or look at the list later in this book for recommendations.

WHAT DOES AUTHENTICITY LOOK LIKE FOR ME?

WHAT IS KINDNESS IN ACTION?

WHAT CAN I DO TO BE SAFE?

WHAT DOES HUMOR LOOK LIKE?

CURIOSITY?

HOW CAN I ACT ACCORDING TO GRATITUDE?

VALVES BRAINSTORM

FIRST, circle (and add your own) up to ten values that guide your actions & decisions.

WORK ETHIC
NATURE
CURIOSITY
PERSONAL GROWTH
FRIENDSHIP
EDUCATION
KINDNESS
NEW EXPERIENCES
HONESTY
MUSIC
THERAPY
FAMILY
ART
SAFETY
SPIRITUALITY
PHYSICAL HEALTH
MENTAL HEALTH
AUTHENTICITY
COMPASSION
INTEGRITY
LOVE
SOCIAL LIFE
ALONE TIME
COMMUNITY
UNITY
ADVENTURE
CAREER
ACTIVISM
PURPOSE
HUMOR
QUIET
STRUCTURE
PHYSICAL ACTIVITY
TRAVEL
JUSTICE
FUN
COMMITMENT
ACHIEVEMENT
LUXURY
CREATIVITY
FINANCIAL STABILITY

ADD YOUR OWN! _____

_____   _____

                    _____

FOCUS ON VALUES

Now, write down those ten values...

1.   6.

2.   7.

3.   8.

4.   9.

                            10.
5.

Next, number those values according to
how powerfully they will guide you
in your daily life. (THIS CAN BE YOUR FIRST
DRAFT, SO NO PRESSURE)

Write the top five here:

1.   3.   5.

                4.

2.

VALUES IN ACTION

HOW WILL THESE VALUES SHOW UP IN YOUR
DAILY LIFE? WHAT ARE YOU DOING OR SAYING
WHEN YOU ARE DEMONSTRATING YOUR VALUES?

WHEN I AM ALIGNED WITH THIS VALUE...	THIS IS WHAT I AM DOING, SAYING, & PRIORITIZING
1.	
2.	
3.	
4.	
5.	

Get Lost in a Book (Or lots of Books)

Reading can be an incredible way to take a step outside of your life for a moment. Whether you're reading non-fiction and learning to do or change something, or fiction that imagines other worlds and possibilities, reading is a great way to take a break from overwhelming emotions.

Here are some of the books I recommend or have referenced in this book:

PEMA CHODRON

When Things Fall Apart
The Wisdom of No Escape
Living Beautifully: With Uncertainty and Change
Taking The Leap
Start Where You Are

BRENÉ BROWN

The Gifts of Imperfection
I Thought It Was Just Me (But It Isn't)
Daring Greatly
Rising Strong

LOUISE HAY

You Can Heal Your Life
Mirror Work
SHE ALSO HAS POWER THOUGHT CARDS THAT ARE REALLY COOL

THICH NHAT HANH

Peace is Every Step

The Miracle of Mindfulness

Anger

No Mud, No Lotus

How to Love

ALBERT CAMUS

The Stranger

The Myth of Sisyphus

CHERI HUBER

There is Nothing Wrong With You

JULIA CAMERON

- The Artist's Way

DR. SEUSS

I Had Trouble in Getting to Solla Sollew

ANNE LAMOTT

Bird by Bird

Hallelujah Anyway

JON KABAT-ZINN

Wherever You Go, There You Are

Coming To Our Senses

Mindfulness for Beginners

STEPHEN HAWKING

A Brief History of Time

ALLIE BROSH

Hyperbole and a Half

SIMONE DE BEAUVOIR

Memoirs of a Dutiful Daughter

The Ethics of Ambiguity

The Second Sex

SHEL SILVERSTEIN

The Missing Piece Meets the Big O

MARIANNE WILLIAMSON

A Return to Love

WORKBOOKS

The Dialectical Behavior Therapy Skills Workbook
  MATTHEW McKAY, PHD.
  JEFFREY C. WOOD, PSY.D.
  JEFFREY BRANTLEY, MD

DBT Skills Training
  MARSHA M. LINEHAN

Recovery of Your Inner Child: The Highly
  Acclaimed Method for Liberating Your Inner Self
      LUCIA CAPACCHIONE, PH.D.

ACT Made Simple
      RUSS HARRIS

The Mindfulness Workbook for Anxiety
      TANYA J. PETERSON, MS, NCC

The Mindful Self-Compassion Workbook:
  A Proven Way to Accept Yourself, Build
  Inner Strength, and Thrive
      KRISTIN NEFF, PH.D.
      CHRISTOPHER GERMER, PH.D.

ANTI-FREAKOUT BOOKSHELF

MAKE A LIST OF ANY OF YOUR FAVORITE BOOKS
THESE CAN BE FROM ANY GENRE, ANY AGE.
(MINE HAS A BUNCH OF CHILDREN'S BOOKS ON IT)

THIS IS YOUR READING LIST! WHAT TOPICS ARE YOU
↡ CURIOUS ABOUT? NEW BOOKS ARE FUN!

CONCLUSION

Sometimes we freak out. That's part of life. It just is. It doesn't have to be embarrassing or shameful to admit that sometimes you just fucking hate your life, or your situation, or yourself, or your friends. It's okay to feel that way. You do not have to let those overwhelming feelings swallow you whole. Instead, you can address your suffering in a way that will help you see your life in the grand scheme. And you can see the largeness of the grand scheme with happiness and peace.

When you're freaking out, the goal is to get back to your peace. You can practice any coping skill that resonates with you and you can see how it works. Remember that every shitty and positive situation is an opportunity to learn and inform future behavior. This isn't about avoiding negative feelings. It's about holding the space for them to exist so that you can feel and move through them.

The last few pages of this book contain space for you to track the coping skills you want to try, and which work best for you. Last is a page to write down everything you need for the moments you're truly freaking out, so you'll always have something from Rational You to bring you back down.

"I am incapable of conceiving infinity, and yet I do not accept finity. I want this adventure that is the context of my life to go on without end." —Simone de Beauvoir

PRACTICE MAKES PROGRESS

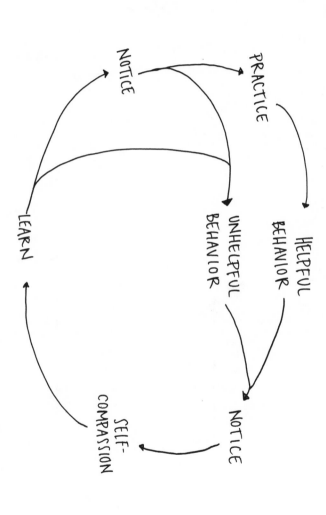

NOTICE

PRACTICE

UNHELPFUL BEHAVIOR

HELPFUL BEHAVIOR

LEARN

NOTICE

SELF-COMPASSION

NEW SKILLS

WHAT SKILLS ARE YOU GOING TO TRY?
WHEN WILL YOU TRY IT? WHAT EMOTIONS
OR SITUATIONS WILL BENEFIT?

SKILL	WHEN TO USE IT

TEN GO-TO SKILLS

I shared my ten coping skills with you.
Now you can choose your own ten!
You can draw pictures, add notes, or just
list them below!

READ THIS

WHAT DOES FUTURE YOU NEED TO REMEMBER, DO, OR SAY IN ORDER TO FIND PEACE?

EVERY MOMENT IS A LESSON

HERE'S A THOUGHT I THINK HUNDREDS OF
TIMES EACH DAY SOLELY BECAUSE OF PEMA CHODRON

EVERY MOMENT IS A LESSON

AS A RESULT—

Shitty moments suck less.

&

I'm much more observant during happy moments

Simone DeAngels (pictured) was born and raised in Austin, Texas, where she lives with her two dogs. In 2012, she entered intense psychiatric care, where she took the tools she learned and made them her own, and made the decision to stay alive. After earning her bachelor's degree in education, she began applying her experience as a patient to her experience as a teacher.

Faith Harper, PhD is a bad-ass, funny lady with a PhD. She's a licensed professional counselor, board supervisor, certified sexologist, and applied clinical nutritionist with a private practice and consulting/training business in San Antonio, TX. She has been an adjunct professor and a TEDx presenter, and proudly identifies as a woman of color and uppity intersectional feminist. TheIntimacyDr.com

SUBSCRIBE TO EVERYTHING WE PUBLISH!

Do you love what Microcosm publishes?

Do you want us to publish more great stuff?

Would you like to receive each new title as it's published?

Subscribe as a BFF to our new titles and we'll mail them all to you as they are released!

$13-30/mo, pay what you can afford!

microcosmpublishing.com/bff

...AND HELP US GROW YOUR SMALL WORLD!

More Five Minute Therapy:

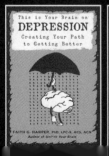

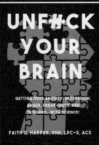